The
Philosopher's
Cookbook

Martin Versfeld

OLDCASTLE BOOKS

This edition published in 2007 by Oldcastle Books Ltd
P.O.Box 394, Harpenden, Herts, AL5 1XJ

Fisrt published in Australia by Figment Publishing

www.oldcastlebooks.com

A CIP catalogue record for this book is available from the
British Library.

ISBN 10: 1-84243-236-2

ISBN 13: 978-1-84243-236-5

2 4 6 8 10 9 7 5 3 1

Printed and bound in Great Britain
by J.H.Haynes, Sparkford, Somerset

Cooking is one of those arts which most require to be done by persons of a religious nature.

A.N. Whitehead

Contents

'Take it and eat,' he said, 'this is my body.'

Matt. 26:26

One should reverence food as the soul (Atman).

Maitri Upanishad 6.12

Tao produced the One.
The One produced the two.
The two produced the three.
And the three produced the ten thousand things.

Lao-Tzu

I

Note on Measures

This isn't a book of recipes or of cooking techniques. It is principally about spiritual food. However, since most books on food seem to be full of measures of time and quantity, I should like to suggest the philosophy of these matters with the help of a few quotations.

The first is from Gulliver's voyage to Laputa, where he tells of a meal with the scientists. 'In the first course there was a shoulder of mutton cut into an equilateral triangle, a piece of beef into a rhomboid, and a pudding into a cycloid.'

This you must connect with the procedure of the tailor making his clothes who 'first took my altitude by a quadrant, and then, with rule and compasses, described the dimensions and outlines of my whole body, all which he entered upon paper; and in six days brought my clothes, very ill made, and quite out of shape.'

The next is from Chuang-tzu[1]:

Ch'ui the draftsman
Could draw more perfect circles freehand
Than with a compass.
His fingers brought forth
Spontaneous forms from nowhere. His mind
Was meanwhile free and without concern
With what he was doing.

(transl. Thomas Merton[2])

Now about time. Cooking is a fine art and not a penance to be got over with as quickly as possible. It should be a linked sweetness, long drawn out. There are occasions — omelets for instance — when speed, never hurry, is called for, but by and large good cooking is slow cooking. The culinary art is corrupted by the widely held belief that time is money. Time isn't money any more than artichokes are angels. The belief is metaphysically monstrous and socially disastrous. If you haven't time for cooking

1 Literally 'Master Zhuang', famous philosopher in ancient China who lived around the 4th C. BC

2 (1915–1968) French-born American Trappist monk and author, now considered by many to be a mystic

you must be poor indeed. The poor man who has not always to be rushing off to the next appointment will often eat best. To get your priorities right, consider this from Chesterton[3]: 'The most precious, the most consoling, the most pure and holy, the noble habit of doing nothing at all.' And this from Dorothy Day[4]: 'The only way to have more time, says Father Lacouture, "is to sow time". In other words, to throw it away. Just as one throws wheat into the ground to get more wheat.'

That gets your fundamental attitude right. You will still have to soft-boil an egg for three minutes, but why boil it in a hurry when you can boil it in eternity, or in 250 millilitres of water instead of in the Sea of Being?

3   G. K. Chesterton (1878–1936), English writer known as the 'prince of paradox'

4   (1897–1980) Journalist turned social activist and reformer, known for her justice campaigns for the poor, hungry and homeless

II

That the Universe Is
the Soup of God

Living as I do in Cape Town, I may be said to owe my origin and location to soup. The settlement of the Cape of Good Hope by the Dutch was prompted by the need for a station for victualling and refreshment on the long and scurvy voyage around Africa to the Spice Islands. Seamen landing in Table Bay would find themselves in a botanist's paradise, and the precursors of the great botanists of subsequent generations were the men gathering herbs and weeds to concoct, perhaps with a bit of salt pork or fish from a teeming coast, a healing soup against the ravages of scurvy. Cooking and medication were, in those days, very closely related, though since the discovery of vitamins we have preferred to draw healing from nature via the drug companies which, in the form of pills and additives, sell us at a great price what grows in our own gardens.

The paradoxical result is that instead of eating well and carelessly we dine in the company of ghosts called kilojoules and vitamins that give money to the shareholders and hypochondria to the many. Kilojoules and vitamins make healthy bank balances for the few, which is why we hear so much about them. Society is riddled with men who have a vested interest in cutting us off from our gardens and making us pay for the re-routing of what nature offers us directly. One shudders to think of the plant life destroyed and the ecological damage done to furnish paper for the advertising boys. Much of health and beauty goes into the medical doctors' wastepaper baskets, which bulge with glossy rhapsodies on something or other with twenty syllables. My grandmother discovered penicillin; she used to apply the mould forming on top of a jar of fig jam to the trouble spot. You probably don't have a jar of fig jam because your figs have been re-routed through the canning companies. The main disadvantage of many old remedies was that they were cheap, whereas a large pharmacist's account is a status symbol, and simple remedies only lessen the prestige of the prescriber as witchdoctor. The old abracadabra cannot compete with the new chemical formulae.

No doubt I am being one-sided, though the accusation will be most loudly made by those who would rather have you live in their blocks of flats than in your own garden. The flat is the outlet pipe of the factory, and when you are deluged with what comes out of it you are in the soup, dehydrated of course, but for that very reason all the more difficult to swim in.

Faithful to my vocation as a part-time cook and scullion in our home I shall presently go and make the soup for lunch. But let me commence by reviewing my resources. With any luck there may be a ham bone in the fridge. I saw Barbara bring in carrots yesterday. Cut on the slant with a Chinese cleaver, they add a touch of lovely colour to the soup. Some barley, which when well cooked gives a creamy texture. Now let's go outside. There are lovage and parsley in the garden, and beyond there are the miles and miles of asphalt with which we tend to cover our erstwhile vineyards and gardens, and which the flat race needs in order to be able to run away from it all at weekends. But nature is a persistent mother, and I do not have to walk a hundred yards to find the soup greens: purslane, very like a portulaca with a shorter, broader, fleshy leaf and a small yellow flower, growing sometimes in the very cracks of the asphalt. Plantain[1] or *tongblaar* (tongue-leaf) is ever with us, cursed by the gardener, but a real gift of God for food and health; when bruised, it can be applied to cuts, sores, bites and stings. The yellow sorrel is pretty ubiquitous, and since the price of onions is again escalating — we live in a society which has escalated even to the moon — try some of the wild onions and garlic to be found in most gardens and most neighbourhoods. You need no more for your soup.

So far, I haven't had much to say about

---

1 *Plantago*, a genus of inconspicuous plants

God. Indeed, He seems to be conspicuous by his absence, precisely because people feel themselves to be so deeply in the soup. If this is history, we don't like being in it. History seems to be a bubbling pot fuelled by the stupidity and iniquity of man, and perhaps we are thinking that if God is the Lord of history he ought to take his blueprint back to the drawing-board. Mircea Eliade[2], in his *Myth of the Eternal Return*, speaks about the terror of history, and there are many who think the terror could be exorcised if we could force upon history a recipe or a programme of our own making. We wish to have it on *our* drawing-boards.

It is important to have the right idea about recipes, and I shall have more to say about them later on in this book. I do not think they are in any way principles of regimentation or formulae for repetition.

Our deep-rooted trouble is that we wish to geometricise everything, to see the universe through a grid. We want to measure and order and straighten out

2   (1907–1986) Romanian historian and writer

and direct so that we can get the better of history. But there are few things as difficult to conceptualise as order. Perhaps it can't be done, because in conceptualising it, we order order, and in this way radically deform it. You can't define the Tao[3] without destroying it. The effect is pernicious, and perhaps especially so in politics. We have heard totalitarian regimes praised for having created order — neat rows of soldiers, police with automatics, and gas ovens to tidy away the rubbish; strong governments that keep the pots of discontent from boiling over.

But neither East nor West, at its deepest levels, has been satisfied with the notion of order as rigidity. Lao-tzu[4] calls this kind of order death, and St Augustine[5] regards

---

3 Taoism refers to a set of philosophical teachings and religious practices rooted in a metaphysical understanding of the Chinese character Tao (literally 'head' and 'go', with a wide scope of meaning depending on the context), encompassing the whole Universe and its processes, considered as constantly changing. You see?

4   6th C. BC Chinese philosopher, reputed founder of Taoism

5 Aurelius Augustinus, Augustine of Hippo (AD 354–430), African theologian and central figure in Christianity and the history of Western thought, best known for his works *The City of God* and *The Confessions*

it as the punitive return of a higher order that has been outraged. How far we are from understanding this we can judge from our reactions to the word 'anarchy.' We have been conditioned to think of an anarchist as a dreadful terrorist with a bomb whose untrammelled explosion upsets our geometric design. But both Lao-tzu and St Augustine have some title to be called anarchists, the former because the Tao runs as freely as water and the latter because the Love of God is the only source of right relationships.

Love, and do what you will, for then your actions will accord with the source of all creation, and marvellously accord with every other action in the whole universe. What Lao-tzu asks for man as a ruler is that he bow out and leave each man to follow his Tao. This will not encapsulate him, but create a state of affairs in which the very rigidities of morality would be transcended, as in St Paul[6] charity

---

6 Paul (originally Saul) of Tarsus or Saint Paul the Apostle (c. 3–67 AD), central to the early development of Christianity and an important interpreter of the teachings of Jesus Christ

transcends the law. Some Zen[7] enthusiasts are far too ready to criticise the law-giving God of the Bible. They have fallen victim to the very legalism they criticise. They have a cheap idea of law, whereas they should have no idea at all, only an openness to the arabesques of nature.

Meanwhile the bits and pieces in our soup pot are performing arabesques on the surface as the water boils. Let us observe them. Certainly there is an order there, an inscape, something like the beating of the sea on the rocks, or a swift eddy in a stream or the wind in the willows. These occurrences are asymmetrical and playful, each moment unique in its 'suchness.' By their very transience they are eternal, and it is the eternal transience which is caught by the decorators of a Grecian urn, or by a Chinese landscape painter, or a good photographer. At every moment there is a new creation, an indication of the surge of the Tao. God is in history and orders things well because they are fluent and

7 Form of Mahayana Buddhism emphasizing enlightenment by the most direct means possible and the value of meditation and intuition

not repetitive. That is why there is a Zen directive to live like a ball on a mountain stream — or a whirling pea in a soup pot — having no care for the morrow, and therefore at the furthest possible remove from the Roman Stoic[8] who killed himself because every day was the same. In the wild dancing of our soup we have the answer to tyrants and iron-fisted regimentators. It is, however, better to view soup without necessarily mapping it out graphically. This is far better, in fact, than throwing bombs. In the soup there is the freedom of God; in the bomb only the cruel freedom of the false anarchist. The true anarchist is the cook allowing the ingredients in his soup pot to be. He is the priest of mutual arising.

Somehow we seem to have got God into the soup, the soup of history, which flows like water, with eddies and curlicues and dreadful plunges. Of course there are soups which are purées, the most interesting part

8   Adherent of the Stoic school of philosophy founded at Athens by Zeno (c. 308 BC) that taught that people should be free from passion, unmoved by joy or grief, and submit without complaint to unavoidable adversity

of which has been left in the strainer. The ingredients have become outgredients. But this is not the soup we are now cooking, with barley corns, orange bits of carrot and dancing green weeds. Our soup is God's soup, swirling and bubbling, all the ingredients remaining themselves and, in so doing, playing their part in the universe which is the pot, an honest soup which has not been mocked up into something which it is not. Clearly, the only way to cope with the terror of history is to realise that no pea is an island, and that it is only by retaining its 'peaness' that it goes along with Tao, uniquely in the soup because dancing in the soup it mirrors forth the One who made it, and in so doing also mirrors forth the 'ten thousand little Ones'[9].

9   'Ten Thousand Things' is a phrase commonly used in Taoist and Buddhist writings to connote the material diversity of the universe

III
Just Soups

Like the rest of this run-down, this is no endeavour to exhaust the subject. Were a volume called *Soups of the World* to appear, I would not be a taker. You should not write about dishes you do not love, or have not lavished care on when preparing, and to pretend to a love of all the soups of the world is to be like the young lady who, when asked about her occupation, replied that she loved all gentlemen the same. It is difficult to assimilate properly the cuisine of even one other country, say Chinese or Japanese. Choose the soup your mother made in preference to Esperanto soup. If you loved your mother, you loved her soups, and of course then the essential ingredients are always to hand. It was my principle, when teaching philosophy, to require my students not merely to regurgitate my soups but to concoct their own.

And 'concoct' is the right word for

the making of soups. You are cooking things together (*con*), and in none of your cooking pots does your world, or what the Chinese call the Ten Thousand Things, come together more harmoniously than in your soup pot. That is why it is so difficult to give recipes for soups; they tend to be an *omnium gatherum* (a gathering of all things) of what's to hand, and you must be in a pretty bad way if you have not the materials for *some* kind of soup. If you have two rashers of bacon, an onion, a handful of purslane leaves — which is a weed in the garden — some barley and noodles, or left-over spaghetti or cold potatoes which you can dice, you are already well away. I remember making one soup — which will never be made again — from three lots of left-overs, each of which was already intricately flavoured. The result was excellent, but I shall never taste it again. For me, making soup is rather like writing; my mind is a ragbag, bits occasionally cohering to form some sort of unity.

When I say that the soup pot is a good place for scraps and left-overs, I do not mean to equate it with the dirt-bin. A soup requires some sense of composition. A cook is very fairly judged by his soups. You must start off a stock pot with good meat and bones, after which it can go on indefinitely if you bring it to the boil often enough to keep it from fermenting.

The soups I most like both to cook and to eat are the thick soups which are meals in themselves, soups you can hail with 'soup of the evening, beautiful soup.' For such soups one should keep a good store of peas, beans, lentils and barley.

I have spoken elsewhere of pea soup. Beans and lentils can also be cooked without meat if given a good dollop of butter. However, most of us prefer meat soup, but the price of meat being what it is, we can get by well enough with stock cubes. The usual local bean soup deserves its popularity.

Soak half a kilo of sugar beans, or butter beans, in warm water overnight. Next day place some pieces of shin, two or three large sliced onions and, if you wish, a couple of chopped chillies, into a large heavy pot and braise lightly, preferably with sheep's fat. Pour the soak off the beans, add them to the pot, fill with water to an inch above the beans and allow to simmer until the beans are very soft. Finally, add salt and, if you wish, pepper. Mashed garlic would not come amiss either, and if you wish your soup to be more velvety, mash some of the beans by ramming the potato-masher into the pot.

By cooking a sufficient quantity of beans you can kill two birds with one stone. You can also make sweet-and-sour beans or *sousboontjies* (sauce-beans). Dish out some beans while they are still whole, add vinegar and brown sugar to them — and if you like, a herb — and bring to the boil. Bottle some, and keep for a cold meal. They go well with salad. In my boyhood it was unthinkable to use any beans other than governor's beans for *sousboontjies*. They were very large, flat, piebald beans that I have not seen around for many years.

Soft-boiled beans can also be deliciously curried and make one of the best vegetarian curries. It is useful to keep a bowl of soya beans in the fridge for such purposes, if you can find a way of getting them soft which is not too demanding of patience and fuel.

Soup of mutton and barley, to which vegetables have been generously added, is always good. Don't forget to add a few cloves, and boil the meat and barley long enough to make the broth creamy and smooth to the tongue. Parsley, celery and chopped shallots improve the appearance. Barley bree can look a bit like a Glasgow winter's morning, so brighten it up by using plenty of carrots and, if you like, sweet peppers in strips.

The method for making thick lentil soup is the same as that for bean soup. Here again there are alternative uses for your soft lentils. Cold, they make a sturdy salad if done up with vinegar and oil, sprinkled with chopped chives and laid on lettuce. Made into a loaf mixed with soaked brown bread and a few eggs, and baked, they make quite a meal. You can add turmeric and curry spices if you wish.

Each of these soups is in itself enough

for a meal. They are not a mere prelude to further eating, unless you are ravenous. A good soup for both purposes is an onion soup. The secret of this is lots and lots of finely sliced onions. Don't be afraid that your breath will smell of onion. It won't. Brown the onions very lightly with a good dollop of butter in a pot, and then add a good brown stock. The soup must be boiled long enough for the onions to disintegrate. Then add salt and black pepper and serve with croutons and grated cheese, preferably a hardish cheese.

A hearty peasant meal of three courses can be had as follows: Brown several slices of shin of beef in your pot, adding some sliced onions. Then pile in such vegetables as you have at hand, cut into smallish pieces and including some diced potato and, if possible, turnips and carrots. Boil till soft, adding celery or lovage.

First course: Marrow from the shin on toast.

Second course: Thick vegetable soup.

Third course: Shin, garnished or with horseradish, or as you please.

The only drawback is in having three courses with the same bouquet, but it makes a very good meal for a hungry family.

There are so many recipes for the thinner soups that I need say little about them. There is nothing to it if you have good stock and a few herbs, especially shallots. Stock cubes are not to be sneered at. Just remember that a dish must point outwards as well as inwards. You have to consider not only the palate, but also the Ten Thousand Things. When you take the lid off the tureen, you should in fact be opening a window onto a garden.

Sherry does well in many of the thinner soups. We keep a bottle of sherry in which a couple of chillies have lain for some weeks. Try a small spoonful in your soup.

Seafood soups are legion, and though here I claim no expertise, I would like to mention a haddock chowder. Braise a little cubed smoked pork in your pot and add chunks of potato and sliced onion, covering them with water. Boil until soft. Steam the haddock until it is soft enough to flake,

flake it and add to the pot together with a tin of evaporated milk and a good nut of butter. Pepper, but don't salt. Add a little chopped parsley and top with a grating of nutmeg and a double handful of broken crackers.

Instead of haddock, take white mussels, well cleaned, and braise them gently with butter, green fennel and shallots. Then proceed as above.

IV

The Divinity of Food

Man has been defined as a rational animal, a laughing animal, a tool-using animal and so on. We would be touching upon a deep truth about him, however, if we called him a cooking animal. He prepares his food. Perhaps a lion prepares its food by reducing it to bite-size chunks with its teeth, but preparation goes a bit further when *homo something-or-other* cuts an animal into bits with a flint knife. Teeth then become less necessary than they once were.

But this is not yet cooking, properly speaking, because that you only have once *homo ignifer* gains mastery over fire and can contain and control it. This was so tremendous an occurrence, adding such a new dimension to what man previously was, that fire came to be seen as either a gift of, or theft from, the gods. Presumably this is the origin of the burnt offering: We give back to God a tooled animal which rises

22

up to him because it is transformed by a divine essence. The Upanishads[1] talk about the digestive fire and tell us to reverence it. The fire on the altar transforms the meat into food for the gods. Immolation is the divine digestion, and God becomes the food and the fire; later, the bread and the wine. Cooking and offering have always gone together.

Food is something we clothe with both a human and a divine aspect. Just as the world of colours is the correlate of man's sensory make-up, so the world as food is the correlate of his oral and digestive fire and his alimentary system. In this sense man creates food, just as his eye creates colour, or a railway train a passenger: no train, no passenger; no man, no food. The world as food is the world humanised. I might not be the bread of life, but I am the life of bread. Food, then, is something spiritualised. There is a difference in kind and degree between what is food for man and what is food for a dog or a praying

1 The Upanishads are part of the Hindu Shruti scriptures which primarily discuss meditation and philosophy

mantis. Man is not only a preying animal but also a praying animal. In the mantis he sees his own benediction. The flesh he eats must be prayed over before it can become not only his body and blood but also his spirit. When you eat bread you also eat reality. When you *see* your plate of dinner you have already enminded it, or assimilated it into that aspect of you which is intelligence. An eaten world is an intelligible world, a world in which body and spirit are united.

And it is fire that has made this transformation possible. No wonder there are fire worshippers, for it is through the cooking fire that man and the world have jointly expanded. It is in the fire under the cooking pot that the presence of God is focused. Where there is a Burning Bush[2], God is near, as He is wherever there are electric or gas stoves, Bessemer[3] converters or power stations. If today we are electricity worshippers rather than fire worshippers,

2 Reference to Exodus 3:2 where God revealed Himself to Moses as flames of fire within a bush

3 Large ovoid steel container lined with clay or dolomite, named after its inventor, Henry Bessemer

it is because we still require a God whom we cannot fathom, but who makes all things tick. It is because Nature is a Heraclitean fire, or if you like a huge atom bomb, that Christ[4] 'plays in ten thousand places.' When Heraclitus[5] says that fire is the creative Logos[6] or intelligencing Word, he is bringing down the barriers between matter and spirit. Each bush that you burn is a holy bush, and whenever you cook a lamb you are a priest.

The umbilical cord between yourself and the world is the cooking pot. We pass reality through it, and it is indicative of the sort of world we live in. It is a crucible, an alembic in which we are linked with the world, magically if you like.

Through it, subject becomes object, and object subject, and ultimately atman[7]

---

4 Jesus Christ, or Jesus of Nazareth, believed by Christians to be the Son of God, their Messiah

5 Pre-Socratic Greek philosopher of Ephesus, 535–475 BC, known as 'The Obscure'

6 Often translated from the Greek into English as 'word' but with various meanings including thought, speech, reason, principle, standard or logic, among other things

7 Individual self, known after enlightenment to be identical with Brahman

because Atman is Brahman[8]. Hence there is something divine about pots, and it was therefore only logical to dedicate a bronze tripod to Apollo[9] at Delphi[10].

There is nothing more indicative of what man is than his pots and their relation to the landscape. It is not surprising that archaeologists are such inveterate pot-gazers.

You have pots, large and small, in many materials: big copper pots, heavy iron pots, some three-legged, a legion of enamel and aluminium pots, clay pots and stainless steel pots, and the whole family of pressure pots which have descended from Papin's digester[11]. The majority of these pots tell you that men were miners, the three-legged pot proclaims that they cooked on open fires, the large ones that

8 Impersonal supreme being in Hinduism with a complex range of other meanings

9 A god in Greek and Roman mythology, son of Zeus and Leto and the twin of Artemis

10 Site of the Temple of Apollo in ancient times and revered throughout the Greek world as the site of the omphalos stone, the centre of the universe

11 Denis Papin invented the 'steam digester', a type of pressure cooker, in 1679

they ate in groups, the stainless steel pots that they were advanced chemists and metallurgists, the pressure pot that they lived hurried lives. The great cylinders of the jam factory tell of mass production and the economy that goes with it. All speak of certain kinds of being together, and of the varying relations of these groups to external nature.

Political science is the science of pots. The jam factory cylinders or cauldrons point to the large orchards outside. They are, as it were, the spectacles through which we see them. Look at the landscape and see how much we need pots to explain it. We humanise the landscape by producing food. All that over there is vineyard, there is an apricot orchard, the misty blue-grey of that hillock is olive trees, here are vegetable gardens and cornfields, and the roads that make the various products available to us. Consider how many roads and shipping lanes lead into your kitchen. And however much this may point to a swollen bank balance or a swollen ego, it also points to a way of living together and giving mutual aid. The food for the body thus creates the food of the soul, which is an understanding of persons. Our knowledge and our virtue are visible in those fields. That landscape is something that *we* made, that we have lifted up to a person. *I* see it because *we* see it. Our very sense perceptions are communal. It is not simply a matter of 'I see a plough', but of 'we see a plough through me.' The plough is history. It took many ages to invent. Only cooperation makes history, and there is a very real sense in which time itself is man-made.

In Catholic[12] belief we partake of God when we partake communally of the bread and the wine which the earth has brought forth and human hands have made. We call down a blessing on the food and offer it as a sacrifice. This is the essential character of sacrificial meals and there is also a sacrificial character in domestic meals, something which was recognised in societies where, before eating, one poured

12 The Roman Catholic Church, with the Pope as its head, is believed to be the original Christian Church

a libation to the gods. The essential point is that the partaking of food is the partaking of reality.

This is very strikingly brought out in the Taittiriya and Maitri Upanishads, where ultimate reality is said to be food. The early Hindu[13] saints and metaphysicians, seeing man as a fragmented bit of reality, sought his reintegration and asked what the nature of the primary reality was in which man sought wholeness. Some said water, some said food. This must not be understood as materialism, in our sense of the word, which depends on a distinction between spirit and matter. That distinction is not hard and fast in the Upanishad thinkers any more than it was for Heraclitus when he said that the ultimate reality, the ultimate wisdom or Logos, was fire. Observe that the Upanishads say: Reverence fire, reverence water, reverence breath, reverence food — which indicates that these elements have a spiritual dimension. The food in us is one

13 Hinduism, commonly called *Sanatana Dharma* (roughly 'Perennial Faith'), the main religious and social system of India, including belief in reincarnation

with the Food, which is therefore seen to have a nourishing and dynamic quality, sustaining not only biological life but also thought and spirit.

> From food, verily, creatures are produced,
> Whatsoever creatures dwell on the earth.
> Moreover by food, in truth, they live.
> Moreover into it also they finally pass
> For truly food is the chief of beings;
> Therefore it is called the essence of all
>   things.
> Verily, they obtain all food
> Who worship Brahma as food.
> For truly, food is the chief of beings,
> Therefore it is called the essence of all
>   things.
> From food created things are born.
> By food, when born, do they grow up.
> It both is eaten and eats things.
> Because of that it is called food.
>
> (Taittiriya Upanishad 2.2)

He who is established in reality 'becomes an eater of food, possessing food. He becomes great in offspring, in cattle, in the splendour of sacred knowledge, great in fame. One should not despise food' (Taittiriya Upanishad 3.8). Hence it is easy to understand why we are told to reverence the digestive fire. Let us say that God is most present at the domestic hearth.

> Oh, wonderful! Oh, wonderful!
>> Oh, wonderful!
> I am food, I am food, I am food!
> I am a food eater, I am a food eater,
>> I am a food eater!
> I am a maker of verses! I am a maker of
>> verses! I am a maker of verses!
> I am the first born of the world-order
> Earlier than the gods, in the navel of
>> immortality!
> Who gives me away, he indeed has aided me
> I who am food, eat the eater of food!
> I have overcome the whole world!
>
> (Taittiriya Upanishad 3.10.6)

The Upanishad ends with the line: 'Such is the mystic doctrine.' It is called a mystic doctrine because he who is established on food is one with ultimate reality, therefore is Brahman and hence no different from this manifold universe, the source of whose dynamic is the sustenance it receives from Brahman as the source of all growth, and nourishment, therefore, as Food.

This doctrine passes through Buddhism[14] into Zen. The Vimalakirti Sutra[15] tells us that when one is identified with the food one eats, one is identified with the whole universe. When we are one with the whole universe, we are at one with the food we eat.

As in the Catholic Mass[16], we eat and drink the Truth, who is a person, the Purusha[17] of the Maitri Upanishad. Brahman is 'the fire in the stomach which cooks food' (Maitri Upanishad 6.18), and through this fire we relate to the fire which is the breath of God as the divine *Logos* or Person with whom we are one. When

14 Widespread Asian religion or philosophy, founded by Gautama Buddha in India in the 5th C. BC, teaching that elimination of the self and earthly desires is the highest goal

15 Scripture considered one of the most profound of the Indian Mahayana Buddhist sutras

16 Celebration of the Eucharist, the Christian sacrament commemorating Christ's Last Supper

17 In Hinduism, the 'self' which pervades the universe

we eat we are the personification of the universe, and to be experientially aware of this is to be enlightened. The whole universe is the whole personified Truth, the eating of which is eternity.

The cook, even the domestic cook, is a priest or priestess, and in a Zen monastery this is realised in the status given to the cook. He must be enlightened to hold the office of *tenzo*[18]. None but the best are good enough for this office, and the *tenzo* should be well on his way to Buddhahood. It is interesting to find that the kitchen priest is required sometimes to devise dishes which will give great pleasure to the community. You cannot handle food properly unless you think highly of its nature, however humble your materials are. You must love water and rice as if they are children to be reared.

It is good to hear that the food should be capable of giving pleasure to the eater, and to contrast this with the attitude of some of

18 A Buddhist disciple who bears the responsibility of caring for the community's meals

our Puritans[19] of whom Macaulay[20] said that they prohibited bear-baiting not because it gave pain to the bear, but because it gave pleasure to the spectators. The Western lay brother who served food which was a burnt offering would not be looked on with an indulgent eye. Being aware of the presence of God in so-called menial tasks is not to have one half of your mind on what you are doing and the other half on God, or to have a rosary in one hand and a soup ladle in the other, but simply to have your whole mind on what you are doing. A well-cleaned, well-cut carrot *is* a praise of God. Your praise consists in bringing out the 'suchness' of your materials. The loving way in which you sort dried peas or peel an onion brings you into touch with Being. If Descartes[21] could say that no atheist could be a mathematician, a Christian or a Zen monk might say that he couldn't be a cook

19 Group of radical English Protestants who sought to simplify and regulate forms of worship

20 Thomas Babington Macaulay (1800–1859), British poet, historian and politician

21 René Descartes (1596–1650), aka Cartesius, philosopher, mathematician and part-time mercenary

either. If you want to convert an atheist, get him to clean the carrots well. To become enlightened or receive grace it is not necessary to sit in the lotus position — into which I could only be forced by a sledge-hammer — but to be peeling potatoes or washing up. And you would not drop the plates either.

Earlier on I asked you to look out of the window at the fields and factories and to realise that primarily it is the production of food which makes us members of one another. Remember that the prime mover in a factory is a direct descendant of the cooking fire, as is all experimental science and technology. Of course, without this we could not be exploiters of one another either. You will get worse food and more expensive food in proportion to the exploit-ativeness of society. But the cardinal point is that as it is primarily food that relates us to one another, so it is food which relates us to God, since we can nowhere find God except in relating to people. To love God and to love our fellows are one and the same act. Christ says that when we give drink to the thirsty, we give it to him. To refuse food to the hungry is an offence to the Christ in the hungry. Even if the fire has been generated by oil or electricity, and the food put in cans, the same truth holds: an industrial system which makes people poor and hungry is an offence against God.

Food being what binds us together in a unity, which is the better in proportion to its proclaiming our union with God, we find ourselves naturally drawn to the idea of a *convivium* or living together. In Latin *convivium* means a meal together, and the Greek *symposium* is a banquet. Where two or three are gathered together to eat the divine food, there God is present. Where the divine food is refused, there will be mutual suspicion, exploitation or the cannibal egoism which creates St Augustine's City of This World, or the Buddhist hell. The mystical level in Plato[22] reaches its greatest heights in *The Symposium* when the priestess Diotima tells of man's union with

22 (*c.* 427–347) Influential Greek philosopher, student of Socrates and teacher of Aristotle, best known for his dialogues, esp. *The Republic*

Beauty. You cannot make Socrates drunk because he has drunk too deeply of the wine of this beauty.

The good life, then, is the convivial life where the atman, or individual soul of John, and that of James, are seen to be One in the Atman because the very universe is one great *convivium* blazing with joy, where the water or wine we drink — and they were the same in God in the marriage at Cana[23] — has not lost its corporeality because it is the eternal drink which will take away all thirst. Hence we talk of tasting life, of tasting God, the gustation of God, when our flesh and blood call for the Living God — our flesh and blood, not a meagre spiritual ego born of desire and abstraction and attempting to nourish itself on the thin soup of 'success.'

23 Biblical miracle in John 2:1-11 where Jesus turns water into wine at a wedding

V

The Daily and the Festive

The distinction between the daily and the festive meal is quite fundamental. It is a distinction which Samuel Johnson[1] made when he said: 'This was a good dinner enough, to be sure, but it was not a dinner to ask a man to.' This would apply to an invitation which was rather formal and to be distinguished from those happy occasions when, on the spur of the moment, we invite a friend to take pot luck. To take a man into your house — or your pot — is to open up your heart to him. Nothing is more indicative of what you are than your food and table customs.

The daily round, the common task, of the domestic cook is to supply something satisfying for a small community. It need be nothing extraordinary, unless something unusual just happened to turn up. Merely something that goes with an

1 Dr Samuel Johnson (1649–1703), English critic, poet, essayist, biographer and lexicographer

ordinary day, the conversation which makes for a shared life, and with a glass of *vin ordinaire*. It can usually be good and interesting, and surprises are very much in order. It is just a matter of making the best of your materials, or making them speak with their true voices. Deep calls to deep, from the centre of good bread and butter to something central in you. This is called enjoyment, and it is much more than sensual. Zen is having this cup of tea, or whatever it is you usually have. A good cook, like any other good artist, seeks to please, that is to make his pigments speak out and reveal what they are. This honest pleasure is somewhat different from high rejoicing. It is gluttonous, perhaps deadly, to want that every day. We can never be festive if we wish each day to be a feast. Where everything is festive, nothing is festive. We would be so accustomed to seeing miracles that we would not see any.

Festive meals are *occasions*. If we acquire, say, a fine haunch of buck, it is an occasion for an occasion. It must be nobly spiced and marinated, friends must be invited, for their pleasure will be ours also, and we can heighten our spirits with some good wine which has ascended, like us ourselves, from the good earth. Or perhaps there is a birthday to be celebrated. Let us pity those who do not wish to celebrate their nativity. We give gifts because we are rejoicing at the greatest gift of all: God's gift of a man to himself. We are refusing to say with Seneca[2]: *Vitam nemo acciperet si daretur scientibus* — nobody would accept life if he knew what he was getting. One recalls Xerxes[3], reviewing his enormous army at the Hellespont[4]. Artabanus, his uncle, asked him how it was possible for him to weep. 'It came into my mind', said Xerxes, 'how pitifully short human life is — for of all these thousands of men not one will be alive in a hundred years' time.' 'Yes,' said Artabanus, 'but there are sadder things in life even than that. Short as life is,

2   Lucius Annaeus Seneca or Seneca the Younger (*c.* 4 BC – AD 65), Roman philosopher, statesman and dramatist

3   Xerxes I (reigned 485–465 BC), Persian King of the Achaemenid Dynasty

4   Hellespont (also called *Rectum Hellesponticum*) was the ancient name of the Dardanelles, after Helle, daughter of Athamas, who drowned there

there is not a man in the world, either here or elsewhere, who is happy enough not to wish — not once only but again and again — to be dead rather than alive . . . God who gave us a taste of the world's sweetness has been a niggard in his giving.' This is what we deny at Christmas[5] and Easter[6], so let these be very great festivities.

There was a great feast when the prodigal son[7] came home. The fatted calf was killed. Indeed, all returns call for festivities. Friends or children come back from far places, and we say: Let us eat and drink together, for in this bread and meat and wine our wholeness is restored.

I am not sure how to deal with most large gatherings. Wedding feasts, however, are firmly rooted in tradition, therefore in human nature. We are *not* sorry to see the human race go on, and the joy of bride and bridegroom suffuses the future with hope

5 Literally 'the Mass of Christ', a holiday in the Christian calendar celebrating the birth of Jesus, usually on 25 December

6 Christian festival commemorating Christ's death, named after *Éostre*, a Pagan fertility goddess associated with spring

7 Biblical parable of Jesus in Luke 15:11-32 in which a lost son returns home and is reconciled with his father

and the present with acceptance. This wine is good.

Large formal occasions and public dinners in general? I know that these, too, are traditional, but I shall be inconsistent and say: Try to turn them down even if you have to say that you are dead, or have piles. Corporations and institutions cannot give. They can only dole out, and this is part of the mutual cannibalism of metropolitan life.

The domestic and the festive, then, are perfectly congruous. The festive expresses more decidedly the idea of largesse. It calls for a certain superfluity: wine in full measure and running over, and a riot of food which makes you goggle. Observe that *superfluous* means running over; it also means unnecessary or more than what is needed. That is why the festive is the godly. Christian sensibility maintains that God was under no necessity to create. The Ten Thousand Things are there and are good because goodness is *diffusivum sui*, diffuses itself. One might say that creation is a sheer boiling or bubbling over of the high spirits of God, as gratuitous as love always is. God is really rather absurd. Are not love and absurdity closely connected? I love dogs and generally find them absurd. My Corgi is quite ridiculous. I suggest that God finds the Ten Thousand Things absurd and ridiculous, especially ourselves. Consider for instance the devices of plants to propagate themselves by seed. Effective adaptations, no doubt, but utility is not their only dimension. Can't you see this uprush of divinity as lovable and absurd? All those hooks and points, flower heads like footballs that roll in the wind, lush fruitiness that tempts the birds and baboons, who then disperse the seed by defecation. To me it is a festive carnival, the participants wearing masks or dominoes because they themselves are the masks of God.

A great number of modern dramas present man as meaningless and absurd. But what if it is our meaning to be absurd — and loved — or to be eternal because we are superfluous? A philosophy which cannot laugh is far removed from reality, and it is one of the marks of the nobility of Zen that it finds itself comic. Perhaps when we find the shortness of our lives to be ridiculous we shall be reconciled to death and at peace with God.

All creativity knows that it is justified by its sheer superfluity. In Charles Williams's[8] *Taliessin Through Logres* the king's poet, Taliessin, says:

'Must I be once more superfluous
as to Dindrane and the kingdom so to the
    company,
verse is superfluous, and I even to verse.'
    Dinadan answered:
'Sir, in the charge at Badon and the taking of
    Camelot,
though you were chief you were still
    superfluous ...
This purchase of modesty is nothing new.
Take the Largess, think yourself the less,
    bless Heavens.'

For Williams our superfluity is an

8 Charles Walter Stansby Williams (1886–1945), English publisher, writer and member of The Inklings, an Oxford literary group that included J.R.R. Tolkien and C.S. Lewis

'excellent absurdity.'

We are here, God *knows* why. But that is the whole point: God knows why. Our existence has no substance other than creative joy. If that is so, then our very substance is humility, and that is the heart of true festivity. That is why the miserific puritanism of Sartre[9] cannot understand festivity. It cannot do so because Sartre has said that Adam created himself.

Festivities, then, celebrate among other things the divinity of food. Wherever you have celebrations in this spirit you have festivities. A festivity does not necessitate all sorts of gorgeous food. You can celebrate on bread and cheese if you hold them in your heart. It is far more essential for the heart to overflow than the dishes. Let that be your superfluity.

Festivities, then, should be in proper season, and are fundamentally domestic occasions. By all means, go to a good restaurant occasionally, if only to show that you have money which is superfluous.

9 Jean-Paul Sartre (1905–1980), French existentialist, philosopher, dramatist, novelist and critic

But cooking and the home are united by inseparable bonds. Homes also have a divinity, linked with the divinity of food. No wonder that your *lares*[10] and *penates*[11], your household gods, are given a place by the hearth. In our farm kitchen a crucifix hangs above the hearth, sharing its nail with things like skewers and ladles. It is by the help of fire that the food becomes me, and it is through fire that the food goes to God. Every act of cooking is a sacrifice, and every house is an altar. Only the love of God can accept as a sacrifice this ready-made stuff embalmed in plastic which you just warm up. Domestic cooking, however, always borders on festivity. In a loving household one is always on the verge of the transformation. What you live in, and what you live on, go together, and, so unified, each is one of the mansions in our Father's house. Heaven is simply being at home with yourself and others, and your eternal mansion is the house you build here.

Material bricks are spiritual bricks.

10 Roman deities protecting the house and the family
11 Also household gods, especially of the storeroom

There is a Zen story of a man of Zen who was visited by a monk who said he came from the Monastery of Spiritual Light. The man of Zen replied: 'In the day we have sunlight and at night lamplight. What is spiritual light?' When the monk could not answer, he said: 'Sunlight, lamplight.' That is the right point of view if you believe in the Incarnation. What is spiritual bread? The loaf in the oven. As a creature it bears the footprints of the Creator, and is that not spiritual enough? The emancipation of women is a thing of great good, as long as it does not divorce the priestess from her altar. That is the way divorces start.

VI

Utensils

Utensils are the media through which things from the outer world are humanised. They are a means by which we touch nature. The ability to humanise things by fire was the beginning of the ascent of man. From it sprang light and cooking, and also the means to extract copper and tin and gold and iron from the rocks. A cooking pot was the first crucible, and the first smiths were regarded as miracle workers who could draw the sword from the stone. A Bessemer converter realises a possibility present in the first man-made sparks, a titanic possibility, a sense of which made men regard fire as a theft from the gods and finally made them persuade themselves they were gods. Mankind has always felt there is something divine about fire, employing vestal virgins to keep a sacred flame perpetually alight so that mankind would not perish. Cooks are the priests and priestesses of the kitchen.

Their pots should smell divinely so that it may be proper to offer a portion to the gods and pour a libation. So let us at the very least say grace before meals and offer to God what we have received through the fire of his glory.

Perhaps we can call fire a utensil on the grounds that it is something we use. We can't cook without it. Indeed, we may think of cooking as the art of bringing certain materials into contact with fire in such a manner as to render them more edible. So we can start with the subject of fire.

Sticks and flints are still used for making fires, which we generally light with lighters and matches these days and which are usually open, or enclosed in a stove. In the concrete jungle there are possibly many children who have never seen a coal and wood stove, or lit a fire of sticks. The open fire came first, and I rather think it has the last word. At any rate, I enjoy cooking over an open fire, standing the pots on an open grid. As a method it owes its superiority to the tang of woodsmoke which gets into your pots. That smoke is a very important spice, you will see, if you try to smoke fish over pine sawdust instead of over oak. If you are cooking in the country you should know your smoke as you know your spices. And by the way, if you are a smoker, don't use matches when sitting by the fire, but rather a spill of the right wood. One uses different woods for different purposes. If you merely want a kettle of hot water, any wood which blazes quickly will do — poplar, for instance, or fir. But for a pot roast or a stew this will not do at all. 'Though the bavin[1] burns brightly, it is but a blaze.' You must know your woods and their various smells. Hardwoods are extremely accommodating and all good campers know which ones burn with a slow, steady certainty that allows you to leave your three-legged pot to cook for hours over a slow reliable heat. The secret of good cooking is generally slow cooking. Get a couple of faggots of hardwood slowly smouldering under your iron pot with the pheasants in it, a pot round which an

1 A faggot of brushwood or other light combustible matter used for kindling fires

occasional curl of aromatic smoke dawdles, and just leave it for hours. Very small coals do for a very long simmer. It is one of the marks of sanctity not to smite with a ladle those well-meaning visitors from town who mess around with your fire; to last out when you see a pile of choice wood disappear rapidly into hands on which there have never been any blisters raised by an axe. It takes years to learn how to make and tend an open fire properly.

Next in order comes the wood and coal or anthracite stove. This is excellent, but out of the question for the millions imprisoned in flats. One of its main advantages is that the temperature varies from one area on the surface to another. It is very efficient as a heater and really comes into its own in the farm kitchen which is also used as a living-room. I heard on a train journey, in somewhat primitive countryside, of the interesting transition from open to enclosed fires. To have had an iron Dover stove was a prestige symbol in the rural areas in the long-dead days of which I am speaking, and in one such country area lived an old couple who had sufficiently emerged from poverty to buy a Dover. Asked how it was working, they said it was working well, only it smoked a bit. It turned out they were making an open fire on *top* of the stove. If this seems incredible to you, I must reply that I see no limits to human stupidity. A small dealer in our neighbourhood was asked by an elderly woman to come and knock in a nail for her, as her husband was unable to do it. My friend found him trying to knock the nail in head first.

The real transition, however, came with the advent of the clay stove, which seems to have been used pretty universally in the old cultures, for instance that of Egypt, when one had to stoke with papyrus. I don't know who first had the idea of knocking a hole in an ant-heap.

But to come back from the bronze age, we seem to have ended up with gas and electric stoves. Of these the former are better because they make possible an instant change in heat and enable you to see what you are doing. Electric stoves are something we have been conned into. Electric ovens, however, are pretty good. Remember that nothing that is mass-produced is ever made for you, being made rather for an abstract individual endowed with standardised tastes. So money is abstracted from concrete human beings, who are regarded merely as abstract bellies staggering around in the supermarket.

Having got your fire ready, you must bring to it your envisaged food. The bringing together may be by way of direct contact, as in the case of spit-roasting and barbecues, but we must not forget that pots were invented at a very early stage. Archaeologists find pottery remnants at very great depths, and these tell them more about man than any other relict because they tell of his relation to the earth and to his fellows. Pots and family life are closely interconnected. *Mater* is matter and matter is clay, of which we are made and to which we shall return. The clay pot embodies our mortality to as great an extent as the columbarium[2].

2 Place for the respectful public storage of cinerary urns

When you buy pots and pans, you are acquiring tools for living. Think big. You do not want your life to be potbound. Pots are better large than small. You want something you can stir robustly with a wooden spoon. Large pots point to children, friends, guests — all those who share your salt with you. Your pots must be able to contain them. Distrust the family whose pots are small.

So much for size. Now for weight. Your pots and pans should be heavy, because heavy ware equably distributes heat. You are less likely to burn the bredie. My own favourite pot is a heavy cast-iron pot, as black within as without. The older such pots are the better. If you are lucky yours may be an heirloom. Iron is a good and healthy metal for cooking. The Romans, to judge from skeletons, suffered from lead poisoning because they used so much pewter. Some people are suspicious of aluminium, so play safe and use heavy enamel. One needs pans, both large and small. If they have lids, so much the better. See that your largest pan has a lid. Here, too, go for weight.

Earthen vessels are, of course, excellent, provided the glaze is free of lead. One cannot imagine an *olla podrida*[3] in a metal vessel. Earthen ovenware is rightly favoured, and it is hardly necessary to mention the utility of oven-proof glass. We have a large stainless steel roasting pan which is highly satisfactory. In fact the advent of stainless steel is, with some reservations, a Good Thing.

Pressure-pots? To be avoided where possible. You can do quite a good second-rate meal in a pressure-pot, but nothing showing any artistry. It is useful for reducing dried peas or beans to something that can be used for cooking, or perhaps to get the better of a tough bit of beef for a soup, but its use does not evoke skill or imagination. It is no substitute for long, slow simmering.

There are two utensils of Eastern origin which are a great spur to one's versatility. The first is the Chinese wok and the

3 Stew of seasoned meat and vegetables, a culinary miscellany

second the Indian chapatti[4] pan. The wok is essential for Chinese cooking.

The wok cannot be used on an electric stove. It can be stood on a gas burner if you make or secure a metal collar on which to place it. This is because a wok has a rounded bottom. It is a shallow, rounded pan of sheet iron with two handles, excellent for paellas[5], stir-frying or what have you. It comes in various sizes. Once you acquire one, you can set out on a long voyage of discovery. You can start with scrambled eggs, and go on to sweet-and-sour pork and vegetables, well cleaned, cut up and quick-fried in the Chinese manner. If you want a lid, get a circular aluminium tray and fix a handle to it.

The Indian chapatti pan also has many uses. It is a heavy iron disc resembling a disc from a disc plough. Because it is heavy, what you cook in it is not easily burnt. It, too, must be stood on an iron collar. It makes excellent griddle cakes. The pan

4 Type of roti or Indian bread, a flat thin cake made with unleavened wholemeal flour

5 Literally 'frying pan' in Valencian, a Spanish rice dish with many variations of ingredients, usually with saffron

must be allowed to go black.

Electric mixers and egg-whisks are by no means to be despised. Chapattis, for instance, require two kneadings of fifteen and ten minutes respectively, and here a dough-hook can be of great help. Labour-saving devices, provided they are not capitulations to mere haste, take on quite another aspect when we reflect that a great deal of the world's cooking has depended on the institution of slave labour. Thus scrubbing abalone[6] for an unconscionable time to get it white presupposed the availability of serfs. Again, when you have spent two hours cleaning an Egyptian goose, it is infuriating to find recipes which take its plucked condition for granted. All the pounding the old cookbooks call for conjure up the image of the old Hottentot[7] woman with a scarf round her head making the brass mortar ring like a bell. Some of the old iron pots — we have one that can hold a sheep — cannot

6   Aka *perlemoen,* highly-valued mollusc of the genus *Haliotis,* lined with mother-of-pearl

7   Term for the Khoi people who were the original inhabitants of the Cape of Good Hope

be handled by an ordinary housewife and require the assistance of someone sturdy. Whoever invented a spice mill did more to abolish slavery than any public meeting ever did. I doubt whether machines reduce the overall amount of work in the world, but they certainly do redistribute it.

However, to get back to tools — first and foremost are your kitchen knives. One might say that the world balances on a knife edge. It was the sharp flaked flint that cut the umbilical cord connecting man with the animals. Every man should carry a pocket-knife, rampant, as the badge of his humanity. I carry one, as my father did before me, and I use it at least a dozen times a day: for sharpening pencils, opening letters, peeling fruit, cutting flowers and so on.

Well, then, kitchen knives: A good knife must be carefully selected, since everything you can buy these days is stainless and frequently will not take an edge. Carbon steel is and always has been much better, but we have been conned out of it and seduced by the glitter of the stainless. Good stainless steel does exist — knives whose edges do not bend over or which are not too hard to be sharpened. I noticed our butcher using a very excellent knife and traced its origins to a firm which supplies professionals: butchers, restaurant chefs and the like.

It is useful to have a small paring knife of about 19 cm. Our most useful knives are about 15 cm in length and are kept very sharp. It is a good index of a knife's sharpness when the edge bites into a tomato skin instead of sliding over it. A longer, heavier knife is most useful too and can also serve as a carving knife. This means bringing a kitchen utensil into the dining-room, which will not please the silver and cut-glass addicts. I like bringing great black pots to the table. Marvellous to take off the lid and let the aroma billow round the company. To appreciate something you need to know how it came to be, which is why Michelangelo left a small area of rough marble on his statues and why a good chef does not mind your sniffing round his pots.

This might be the place to remark that a kitchen need not be as clean and shining as an operating theatre. The sellers of detergents and abrasives have climbed onto the anti-microbe bandwagon, by exploiting post-Pasteur fears. It is salutary to call to mind that only a very deserving microbe would survive simmering for three hours. I grew up in kitchens with dung floors across which farmyard chickens would wander and on which they would deposit their small contributions. I have also had my shocks, as when with a flourish I brought an oven dish of baked galjoen[8] to the table, lifted the lid and found the galjoen garnished with my pipe. I must admit, however, that I do not blame a friend for leaving an Italian hotel after having looked into the yard on a hot and sweaty day and seen the chef shaping rissoles[9] with both hands on his bare torso. But it is more important for a knife to be sharp than for it to glitter, and how much

8 Black bream or blackfish (*Coracinus capensis*), a kind of marine fish found only along the coast of S. Africa

9 Small croquette, usually rolled in breadcrumbs and baked or fried, most often made of minced meat or fish and spices

friendlier a real kitchen table than one with a plastic top!

However, we were talking about knives before we were interrupted. They must be kept sharp, so have a whetstone handy. Avoid like the plague those patent sharpeners that rip off six months' wear with every sharpening. One doesn't treat a friend like that if one wants it to become an old friend. The only knife in our kitchen for which I cannot raise a spark of affection is a serrated bread knife. It has been supplanted by one with a wavy edge, to which I was irresistibly attracted when it cut my thumb as I was testing it.

Some cooks insist on a cleaver, which is all right if you keep a good edge on it, and keep your fingers out of reach! A genuine Chinese choy doh[10] has no parallel. But you can dismember poultry quite well with a heavy knife that is tapped with a meat mallet. If at first you are ham-handed in using the choy doh, you soon won't be! Drop it and you may become a Pobble[11].

10 Knife that looks like a butcher's cleaver
11 From Edward Lear's 'The Pobble Who Has No Toes'

From knives one can move on to spoons. One needs a good, big stainless steel spoon with a handle for supping with the devil! Also, a few other spoons of various sizes. Wooden spoons are friendly things, perhaps because they are made of wood and therefore show signs of wear. For stirring jam there is nothing as good as an old wooden spoon slightly worn at the tip. There are also quite useful plastic spoons in jolly colours. Metal spoons burn the taster's lips.

There are also those gadgets that keep you happy if you have the instincts of a collector. What is better than a knife, for some purposes, is that little vegetable scraper with the slotted, movable blade. It is especially good for root vegetables, though for new potatoes nothing can beat a pot scourer. Peeling potatoes with a knife is wasteful and therefore sacrilegious. A waste economy is ungodly and therefore anathema to cooks or very honest men.

And that is enough about utensils. What it all boils down to is this: stuff that you can love. As Martin Buber[12] has written: 'Around each man — enclosed within the wide sphere of his activity — is laid a natural circle of things which, before all, he is called upon to set free. These are the creatures and objects that are spoken of as the possessions of this individual; his animals and his walls, his garden and his meadow, his tools and his food. In so far as he cultivates and enjoys them in holiness he frees their souls. For this reason, man must always be compassionate towards his tools and all his possessions.'

Do you get that? It takes a saint to be a cook.

12 (1878–1965) Renowned Jewish philosopher, story-teller and pedagogue, born in Vienna but moved to Jerusalem in 1938

VII

Recipes

The nature and function of recipes is not all that easy to determine. We talk about recipes for cooking, for writing books, for cooking uranium or for longevity, and one might even say that the Americans have a recipe for getting to the moon. Let us call a recipe an instruction for attaining a specific effect. It is something which enables a specific end or result to be duplicated an indefinite number of times. In cooking it means: Carry out this or that operation with these or those materials and you will get this or that dish. By sticking to the instructions you can get the same dish ten thousand times over.

Some cookery books are simply an impersonal and classified collection of such instructions which endeavour to be so exact as to make computerised cooking possible. You set the dials and, hey presto, you have a Christmas pudding which you can keep, or put into thousands of tins, all with the same label: Martin's Unique Christmas Pudding, According to a Traditional Recipe of Colonel Wenceslaus[1]!

How you feel about this depends on your attitude to the repetitive and the stereotyped, and here one is likely to land up in the realm of metaphysics. On the one hand nature demands the repetitive. We're all for having the sun rise every morning, having our hearts thump steadily on, having electric switches come up to expectation and finding the newspaper in the letter-box every morning. On the other hand, we do want it to be a newspaper. We expect something new. It had better not be the same paper today as yesterday, though we may want it always to be the *Times*. Curious, since times change, yet we may want to sieve the news through the same old *Times*, even though the news merely illustrates that the imbecility of politicians remains the same, world without end, amen. So closely are repetition and change intertwined.

1 The Patron Saint of Bohemia who encouraged Christianization, martyred by his brother Boleslav

Change rests upon repetition. If your heart did not go on beating the same as ever, you would never be capable of a change of heart, which would involve your behaviour not being the same any longer. It is the tick-tock of time that makes eternity possible for us. Sometimes we allow the tick-tock to invade our idea of everlasting life and arrive at a notion of immortality as an endless tick-tock. We should be hoping for hell, since this is what a never-ending tick-tock would be — a sort of Chinese water torture[2].

Though we always need a pattern, however, we must sometimes have novelty of pattern too. A poet who kept on repeating himself, or created in accordance with a formula, would forgo our admiration; the same old moral saws cease to have any bite; the same old jet aircraft lunch is only tolerable because we don't eat it every day on *terra firma*. Imagine having that lunch every day!

2   Method of torture in which water is slowly dripped onto the victim's forehead, driving them insane; it is unclear whether this form of torture was ever used by the Chinese and the term may be linked to Harry Houdini's Chinese Water Torture Cell (*c.* 1913)

So we accept the cosmic dimension of repetition, however firmly we may reject damnable iteration. The universe itself has a history, and God himself is eternal, not static. His eternity is not frozen time, and the effect of His presence on things is to unfreeze them. You can try this on yourself: To freeze is eternal death.

But, to return to our mutton: Recipes or, if you like, formulae are necessary for the mass production of food, and this accounts for its lack of distinction. For repetition to be at all profitable it must appeal to something purely conceptual, the Average Taste. You cannot risk any deviation because you cannot risk producing something which some people like and others not. There must be no adventure in your tins. The idea is to get everybody liking the same thing for a long, long time. Your next tin of canned seal, made to the recipe of an Inuit[3] nobleman, must be the same as the last if you are to reap optimum profits. The time comes when you con the

3 General term for the indigenous peoples of the Arctic who are descended from the Thule

Inuit himself into preferring the canned product to the fresh one.

Repetitive eating is an interesting phenomenon. The poorer strata of some societies are content to subsist entirely on rice, or beans, or maize. Karen Blixen[4] mentions that her African chef, who cooked well enough for royalty, preferred to exist on simple African staples. I have sometimes asked myself whether there are four foods on which I could happily subsist for all my days, and my answer is yes: dates, bread, mutton and cheese. However, *que sais-je* (what do I know)? I can eat carrots every day of the week, but not parsnips, though I really like them better. It is difficult, also, to gauge the importance of surprise. Institutional food — say at a boarding school — which is served up in repetitive weekly cycles, may be very good in the abstract, but will fail to please because 'we always know what we are going to get.' A little imaginative play each week with herbs and spices might make all the difference.

4   The author of *Out of Africa*, a.k.a. Isak Dinesen

Recipes are not sacrosanct, though there are some noble classics we may look forward to repeating as we do a wine of good vintage. Always remember that it is not simplicity which turns one off. One can enjoy plain brown bread every day; it is the very simplicity which makes the repetition possible. I remember a meal for which our host threw the contents of tin after expensive tin into the pot. A poor family could have lived for three days on what that cost, but I can't remember the taste of the concoction. On the other hand steamed galjoen with butter and lemon has a classical simplicity of which one never tires.

For complexity — classical in another sense — try this one from Apicius[5]:

'Sucking-pig: Bone the pig from the gullet so as to make a sack. Stuff it with meat from a chicken cut up in pieces, thrushes, fig-peckers, force meat made of the pig's entrails, Lucanian[6] sausages, stoned dates,

5 1st C. Roman and author of *De Re Coquinaria* (*On Cookery*)
6 Lucania was an ancient district of southern Italy, now in the modern province of the Basilicata

dried bulbs, snails taken out of their shells, mallows, beets, leeks, celery, boiled cabbage, coriander, peppercorns, pine kernels; finally put in fifteen eggs and *liquamen*[7] mixed with ground pepper. Sew it up and brown. Then roast in the oven. When done, cut it open at the back and pour over the following sauce: pounded pepper, rue, *liquamen*, *passum*[8], honey, a little oil. When boiling thicken with cornflour.'

Apicius, who was a millionaire, committed suicide when he found that he could no longer eat in the fashion to which he was accustomed, and this brings us to the subject of having good things more than once, thus opening the door to gluttony. This becomes a real problem in a society which depends on machine duplication. Duplication obviously has its points for without it there would be no motor spares — presupposing, of course, that you regard cars as a good thing. As

7   Sauce made from rotting fish
8   Sweet wine sauce made by boiling the must

Seneca remarked of wives, you can't live with them and you can't live without them. But the higher one climbs up the spiritual ladder, the more clearly is the attribute of uniqueness seen. You can't duplicate poems, you can't duplicate poets and you can't duplicate God. Sometimes a writer is asked 'When are you going to give us another book like your last?' And if he has any poetry in him, he will say 'Never.' A visitor to Masada[9] recently told me that they would never return. The first impact was enough.' Never another toast from this glass. These chocolates are delicious, and because of that I shall stop at two. The Roman *vomitorium* was a place where you went to kotch up what you had eaten in order to begin again. We have all sorts of *vomitoria* — taking aphrodisiacs, for instance, to rid us of our satiety. However, if you expect every act of sex to be an atomic explosion, you are bound to have a fall-out. Divorce courts are merely *vomitoria* where one disgorges one's previous partner when

9   Mountain-top fortress in east Israel on the south-west shore of the Dead Sea. Site of the Zealots' last stand against the Romans during the revolt of AD 66–73

one is fed up to the teeth with him or her.

Thus we are brought to the perennial philosophical paradox of the same and the different. Philosophising has to do with the everyday and it makes it wonderful. If a philosopher makes you scrabble with your paws at an ivory tower, he is no philosopher. He would have done better at being a politician, since they are past masters at taking the wonder out of life. When you hear a politician preaching principles and ideals, scram! As Chuang-tzu said, well over 2000 years ago:

Hence if you want to hear the very best
     speeches
On love, duty, justice, etc.,
Listen to statesmen . . .
By ethical argument
And moral principle
The greatest crimes are eventually shown
To have been necessary, and, in fact,
A signal benefit to mankind.

(Chuang-tzu 9.2)

Take for instance Hoover's[10] fatuous remark on prohibition: 'A great social and economic experiment, noble in motive and far-reaching in purpose.' It reached far enough to give the green light to Al Capone[11] and get Hoover himself elected.

You will find a very concise expression of the problem of the same and the different in the Hasidic[12] tales.

'When Rabbi Noah succeeded his father, Rabbi Mordecai, to leadership, his disciples noted that in several matters he acted not as his father had done, and asked him about it. "I act," he replied, "exactly as my father did. He never imitated others, and neither do I."' You see? 'She cooks like an angel: impromptu.' If the universe is food, as the Upanishad says, you will find that the Divine Chef excels himself all the time. There are classes of things which look the same, for instance oak trees; yet among the

---

10 Herbert Clark Hoover (1874–1964), mining engineer, humanitarian and 31st President of the USA

11 Alphonse Gabriel Capone (1899–1947), aka 'Scarface', famous American gangster from the 1920s and 1930s

12 Hasidic Judaism, mystic movement founded by Rabbi Israel ben Eliezer (1700–1760), aka Baal Shem-Tov, in the 18th C.

countless trillions of their leaves, no two are the same.

Let population explosions come and go, but there will never be two John Smiths. I suspect that there will never be two pots of bean soup quite the same either. The furthest you can get from the likeness to the Chef is that mass-produced stuff in tins, abstracted from place, time and season, something Eternity never does. We were once taken by a much-travelled lady to a club for the rich. Let me not, with shuddering pencil, have to describe its decor, but you will gather what it was like from our hostess's remark: 'Isn't this wonderful! You could be anywhere in the world.' That's what airports do for you, though we do seem to be reaching the stage when we'll have to go to China to eat Cape abalone. The only time I ever bought Roodeberg[13] over the counter was in a hamlet in the woods of Canada. Just see how simple it is! If God created the Ten Thousand Things in his own image, that

13 Literally 'red mountain', KWV's celebrated blend of noble red grape varietals

is precisely why they are not all the same, but different — they each and all mirror the Unique. To imitate Christ you must be different from him. A world of identical Christs would be pretty hellish. 'If you see a Buddha, kill him,' a Zen master said. Perhaps the best atheist propaganda is tinned beans. They stand very close to canned Christianity, canned Capitalism[14] and the rise of non-religion.

Having got onto the subject of food and morals, I am finding it hard to stop. Is there not something morally oblique about the bad cook? Same question: Why does a Zen monastery require its cook to be an enlightened monk, high up in the monastic pecking scale? Presumably to make the novices feel peckish.

Let us revert to Chuang-tzu:

> With wood from a hundred-year-old tree
> They make sacrificial vessels,
> Covered with green and yellow designs.

14 Economic system in which the ownership of means of production and distribution of wealth is maintained by capitalists, private individuals or corporations, for the making of profit

The wood that was cut away
Lies unused in the ditch.
If we compare the sacrificial vessels with the
    wood in the ditch,
We shall find them to differ in appearance:
One is more beautiful than the other
Yet they are equal in this: both have lost
    their original nature.
So if you compare the robber and the
    respectable citizen
You will find that one is, indeed, more
    respectable than the other
Yet they agree in this: they have both lost
The original simplicity of man.

(Chuang-tzu 9.2)

Chuang-tzu means that it was respectability, that is the Establishment, which crucified Christ between two robbers. Extremes meet — the establishment was the greater robber in taking the life of an innocent man. The priests did not realise that they themselves were the crucified robbers, but Christ knew what he himself was. The penitent thief was promised Nirvana because he recognised the

Buddha nature in Jesus and so was joined so closely to him that their community in death meant community in Paradise. Moralism, as opposed to morality, creates the respectable. Moralism is doing what the Joneses do, that is not knowing at first hand what one is doing; and because the Joneses are voters, they dictate what the Hoovers will say, and vice versa. This is what is called the consent of the governed. A platform is a recipe. Beware of statesmen with principles. They enrich the soil for the unprincipled. On this point the Taoist masters and Nietzsche[15] are at one, although the latter confounded morals and moralism, which the former did not.

So be careful not to democratise your cooking. No two dishes, like no two men, are alike, and it is ungodly to say they are. Governors are kept in power by those who cannot govern themselves, that is by those who have lost their original nature. Society tempts us into masking ourselves from our true selves. How terrible to think

15 Friedrich Wilhelm Nietzsche (1844–1900), influential German philosopher, psychologist and philologist

of a cabinet meeting at which all those present wear masks, and what a macabre ballet you can produce round this theme! Beware of the *Deus ex machina*[16], the God produced by the machine: the voice of the people trimmed and mass-produced to uniformity, proclaiming itself the voice of God.

The chief use of a recipe is to spark you off doing something for yourself. Perhaps this does not apply to the complete beginner, who has still to find out what certain herbs and spices taste like. After all, Van Gogh[17] copied other people's paintings for many years before his genius burst through. You cannot make a paella or a biryani[18] before you have learned not to burn the rice. You are fortunate if in childhood you could watch a good cook at work. How well I remember those farm kitchens: dung floor, black wood stove, gleaming pots, all spick

16 A god introduced into Greek and Roman dramas to resolve the entanglements in the plot; extended to refer to any quick-fix resolution to a problem

17 Vincent Willem van Gogh (1853–1890), Dutch artist, considered one of the greatest European painters

18 Originally an Indian dish made with highly seasoned rice, and meat or fish, etc.

and span, and the smell of roasting coffee and sheep's head and trotters with cloves and onions.

However, you should be able to create something for yourself, something which speaks from you to those you are trying to please. Perhaps you want to please your guests by re-creating some classical dish, say roast beef. But there is more to re-creating than copying. Tradition also inspires, and in any event, I should define tradition as an abiding capacity for change: *change*, not substitution. The resurrection of the dead is creative, if anything is. But the new must resemble, and be a continuation of, the old, or else you have mere revolution. You must be able to satisfy expectations.

My point is that cooking must evoke some spontaneity.

The conditions for good cooking are something like the conditions for good writing. You must know, in some fecund and global manner, what you want to say, but the result should hold some surprises for you. You must love what you are doing, but you cannot love what holds no surprises for you.

Hence a good dish is like a good moral action — something has popped up into it from that mysterious being, the person. Morality by the letter of the law, by unbending principle, or ideal, is destructive. One must avoid cooking by canon law. You should be able to recognise a good cook by his dish, as you can recognise a great writer by any of his paragraphs. They express his essential liberty. Hence a really efficient tyrant should send all good poets and all good cooks to some Siberia[19]. One must be careful about copying even oneself, since the self one is copying is dead, and repetition would be spiritual suicide. So while you are cooking, *compose*. But remember that nobody can be spontaneous unless he has a firm footing somewhere. A *Nataraja*[20] is all change and all equilibrium. If you cannot step into the

19 Region in northern Asia extending from the Ural Mountains to the Pacific Ocean, used by various Russian regimes to punish and neutralise political opponents

20 (Sanskrit: Lord of Dance) In Nataraja sculpture Shiva represents apocalypse and creation as he dances

same river twice, because the water has flowed away, equally you cannot cook the same dish twice. You and those you are serving will have altered in the interim. One can live when one knows how to die, and one can cook when the past feast does not tyrannise the present one. Apicius did not know how to die. Had he known, he would have realised that the highest skill is to take cheap and simple things and bring out their true nature, that is to introduce them to themselves. What death says is: Meet yourself!

This creativity is not enslaved by those precise measures which seem to infest domestic science manuals. Remember that you are practising cooking and not domestic science. Here science is, of course, a misnomer. 'Take 15.5 mm of green ginger and three scruples[21] of salt. Cut across your leeks at an angle of 46°.' That is the sort of thing that happens in a culture obsessed with the quantitative. My beloved Mrs Buwei Yung Chao[22] writes: 'The Chinese

21 Unit of apothecary weight, about 1.3 grams or 20 grains

22 Dr Buwei Yang Chao, the author of *How to Cook and Eat in Chinese*, first published in 1945, is generally credited with the creation of the term 'stir-frying'

cook or housewife never measures space, time, or matter. *Hse*[23] just pours in a splash of sauce, sprinkles a pinch of salt, does a moment of stirring, and *hse* tastes the frying-hot juice out of the edge of a ladle, perhaps adds a little amendment and the dish comes out right.' Try a feather of cinnamon, a grating of nutmeg, a few almonds, a flicker of mace[24] — so much more poetic and therefore suitable, and in a very real sense, more precise.

I insist on the poetic, because cookery is a creative art. It has been said at various times by various people — and has always been true — that every human being is an artist. All of us need some creative activity to defuse our neuroses. It is up to the housewife to seize the opportunity, since cooking is an opportunity so widely distributed. Many women, or men, would cease to complain of being housebound, or unable to make a mark in the world, if they realised this. Sanctity seeks to be unknown, and if you say you have no wish

23 Gender-neutral term for he/she coined by Prof. Yuen Ren Chao, Dr Chao's husband

24 Dried outer covering of the nutmeg, used as a spice

or aspiration, or capability in a specific field, it must be replied that you may, *nolens volens* (whether unwilling or willing), already be a saint or aspiring to be one, since genuine sanctity is unrecognised, especially by the saint himself.

And do not let the transience of your creation get you down — here this morning and gone at lunchtime! A performance of music, or the reciting of poetry, is even more fleeting. It dies on the air. Transience is a fundamental note of ourselves and our world. We are here, and then gone like almond blossom, or the wake of a ship. If you are at home with yourself you will recognise this, and be pleased your art is true to the human condition. Perhaps it is better to be a mayfly than a pyramid. Who knows, said Sir Thomas Browne[25], whether the best of men be known? We must not put our trust in sweet consistencies. 'In vain do individuals hope for immortality, or any patent from oblivion, in preservations below the Moon.' In fact, we have to battle

25 (1605-1682) English author of works in diverse fields including medicine, religion, science and the esoteric

against security, against things that stay put. We dislike artificial flowers because they do not open and die. That is why we bury people with a prodigality of real flowers, hoping the dead have sufficiently cast off their artificial selves to be eternal.

Postscript

I shall now have the sauce to eat my words: I give you the recipe for what I was cooking whilst writing the last pages of this chapter, and suggest it is worth imitating, for I came by it through imitation. It is descended from classical dhal, and its grey hairs deserve respect.

Pea soup: Put half a kilo of soaked split peas into a pot together with a ham bone or some shredded bacon fat — mutton fat does very well too — a teaspoon of turmeric, and two large leeks, chopped up, tops and all. Boil gently until the peas become a purée. Cut up two cloves of garlic, or as many as you fancy, two dried red chillies, and a medium onion, fry them in a little oil and add them to the peas with salt and pepper, raising them to a brief boil. A sprig of mint will not go amiss.

VIII
To Meat or Not to Meat

'Then [the priests] kicked the bodies [of the sacrificed] victims down the steps and the Indian butchers who were waiting below cut off their arms and legs and flayed their faces, which they afterwards prepared like glove leather, with their beards on, and kept them for their drunken festivals. Then they ate their flesh with a sauce of peppers and tomatoes.'

(Bernal Diaz[1])

The traditional association of peppers and tomatoes persists in Mexican lobster.

'(The Argippaei) are said to be bald from birth, women and men alike, and to have snub noses and long chins; they speak a peculiar language, dress in the Scythian fashion, and live on the fruit of a tree called ponticum — a kind of cherry — which is

1 Bernal Diaz del Castillo (c. 1492–1581), Spanish conquistador who wrote an eyewitness account of Cortés's conquest of Mexico

about the size of a figtree and produces a stoned fruit as large as a bean. They strain the ripe fruit through cloths, and get from it a dark-coloured juice which they call *aschy*. They lap the juice up with their tongues, or mix it with milk for a drink, and make cakes out of the thick sediment which it leaves . . . These people are supposed to be protected by a mysterious sort of sanctity; they carry no arms and nobody offers them violence; they settle disputes among their neighbours, and anybody who seeks asylum amongst them is left in peace'

(Herodotus[2])

'I have been assured by a very knowing American of my acquaintance in London, that a young healthy child well nursed, is at a year old a most delicious, nourishing and wholesome food, whether *Stewed*, *Roasted*, *Baked* or *Boiled*, and I have no doubt that it will equally serve in a

---

2 Ancient Greek historian who lived in the 5th C. BC, famous for his writings on the conflict between Greece and Persia, now recognised as a pioneer in history, ethnography and anthropology

Fricasie[3] or a *Ragout*[4].

'Infant's flesh will be in season throughout the year, but more plentiful in March, and a little before and after for we are told by a grave author and eminent French Physician, that *Fish being a prolific Dyet*, there are more children born in *Roman Catholic Countries* about nine months after Lent, than at any other season: Therefore reckoning a year after Lent, the markets will be more glutted than usual, because of the number of Popish infants is at least three to one in this Kingdom, and therefore it will have one other collateral advantage by lessening the Number of Papists among us.'

(Swift[5])

3   Usually spelt 'fricassee,' a dish of stewed or fried pieces of meat served in a thick white sauce

4   Highly-seasoned dish of meat cut into small pieces and stewed with vegetables

5   Jonathan Swift (1667–1745), Anglo-Irish satirist, most famous for *Gulliver's Travels* and *A Modest Proposal*, his controversial essay in which the narrator proposes to fatten up Ireland's undernourished children and feed them to the rich land-owners

IX

At the Sign of the Shrieking Mandrake

There is a well-known dictum of Feuerbach[1], often quoted with superficial levity: *Der Mensch ist was er isst* — man is what he eats. It sticks because it is a good pun, but it is usually quoted at the level of flippant materialism. It is quite easy to depict any animal as an eating machine. Take my dog: a cylinder round a tube with organs at one end which find and ingest food, and at the other end organs to eliminate what is left of the food when the cylinder has had what it needs. At four corners there are little spokes which convey the cylinder, and eyes and a nose to direct it. But somehow this won't do. Taffy has a *name*, because he has joy and humour and affection and content, which are more than mere references to nutrition.

---

1 German philosopher and anthropologist whose major work, *The Essence of Christianity* (1841), maintains that religion and divinity are projections of human nature

The philosophy of Feuerbach did much to unite body and spirit, and if that seems indicative of materialism, let us remember that it is equally applicable to the Incarnation[2] and Resurrection[3]. Of course man is what he eats. If he eats corn he is not a nomad but lives in settlements sharing an agrarian religion with his fellows. If he eats whale meat he must have the technology to build ships and exercise a high degree of cooperation. If he eats tinned fruit . . . and so on. There is no surer clue to what he is than what he eats. When I become the caviare that I eat, it is not by putting on a couple of grammes more weight, but by becoming a *Feinschmecker*[4]. It is equally true to say: *Der Mensch ist wie er isst* — man is how he eats — in the company of his family, with grace before meat, with humour and good conversation. *Mann ist*, man is, he has reality, he has the mystery

---

2 Literally means 'enfleshment', the doctrine that the second person of the Trinity assumed human form in the person of Jesus Christ; concept also employed by Hinduism, Buddhism and other belief systems

3 Rising from the dead, especially that of Jesus Christ

4 Epicure, a person with refined tastes, esp. in food and drink

of existence, and the Taittiriya Upanishad says that reality is Food:

> But food is the chief of beings,
> Whence it is called the elixir of all things.
> Whoso reverences Brahman as food
> Gains all food.

You can interpret Feuerbach material-istically, but you can also slant his dictum towards mysticism.

The Bible got in before Feuerbach when it said: *All flesh is grass*, upon which I give you the commentary of Sir Thomas Browne in the *Religio Medici*[5]:

> 'All flesh is grass, is not only metaphori-cally but literally true, for all those creatures we behold are but the herbs of the field, digested into flesh in them, or more remotely carnified in ourselves. Nay, further we are what we all abhor, Anthropophagi[6] and Cannibals, devourers

5 'The Religion of a Doctor', published in 1643, was a European bestseller in its day

6 Literally 'man-eaters' in Greek, creatures from English folklore with no heads, a mouth in their chests, eyes on their shoulders and diminutive brains in their groins

not only of men, but of ourselves; and that not in an allegory, but a positive truth: for all this mass of flesh which we behold, came in at our mouths: this frame we look upon, hath been upon our trenchers; in brief, we have devoured ourselves.'

Sir Thomas Browne opens for us the themes of autophagy and anthropophagy, which should be explored rather than merely shrugged aside by our prejudices. One might divide the field into culinary and cultural man-eating, though there are points of overlap. It is so wide-ranging a phenomenon that many volumes could perhaps be written about it. I have no cookbook with a recipe for ragout of small boy, though Medea[7] may have possessed one. There are various tales of men being served a dish of their own children by tyrants, the motive being one of sheer iniquity and the recipes left unrecorded. No De Quincey[8]

7 In Greek mythology Medea was the daughter of King Aeetes of Colchis, niece of Circe; known as a sorceress, she assisted her husband Jason in obtaining the Golden Fleece and when he deserted her she killed her children

8 Thomas de Quincey (1785–1859), author of *Confessions of an English Opium-Eater* and *On Murder As a Fine Art*

has written on anthropophagy as a fine art.

In our country there seems to be little cultural evidence of cannibalism. I believe there was cannibalism in the regions devastated by the armies of King Shaka[9] and Mzilikazi[10], the meat doubtless being roasted à la Cyclops[11]. There has of course been a tradition of ritual murder, but the motive for that has not been gastronomic, but rather an endeavour to acquire, by transference, the virtue of the victim. The crudest example of the purely gastronomic that I am able to recall is the ghastly story, from 18th century Scotland, of a large family living in a sea cave and subsisting for years on travellers. Melville's[12] cannibals

---

9 (c. 1781–1828) Also 'Chaka', formidable Zulu chieftan and general in southern Africa

10 (c. 1790–1868) Literally means 'the path of blood', Southern African king and military leader who was initially one of Shaka's advisers and later founded the Ndebele kingdom in what is now Zimbabwe

11 Race of giants with a single round eye in the middle of the forehead

12 Herman Melville (1819–1891), American novelist, essayist and poet, best know for his masterpiece, *Moby Dick*; *Typee* was his first novel, based on his experiences after having jumped ship in the Marquesas Islands

in *Typee* seem simply to have been fond of a bit of roast, and the author's horror at this is simply explained by his revulsion at the idea of himself being the *corpus vile*. There are varying degrees of dislike at the thought of humans being eaten. We don't even like the thought of cadavers being cut up in the interest of medical science. Herodotus remarks: 'It is wholly contrary to Egyptian custom to allow dead bodies to be eaten by animals; that is why they embalm them — to prevent them from being eaten in the grave by worms.' Though at the other end of the scale there is the Tibetan manner of disposing of the dead. The body is taken out of the town and dismembered, by professionals of low caste, for predators to consume.

In all this there is nothing sybaritic[13], which does not seem to have been the case in the South Seas. There long pig, wrapped in banana leaves, cooked in an earth oven and served with vegetables, was regarded as a delicacy. One chief might send a couple of plump children to another chief, much

13 Devoted to luxury and sensuous pleasure

as we might present a brace of pheasants to a neighbour.

There was a curious combination of the religious and gastronomic among the Aztecs[14], who made war for the purpose of obtaining victims for human sacrifice. The capital alone required ten thousand victims a year. On the top of the pyramid, in front of the shrines, was a hog-backed stone on which the victim was stretched so that the priest could sever his ribs with a flint-knife and tear out his beating heart as an offering. The culinary side of it is described as follows by Bernal Diaz:

'A little apart from the *cue* [sacred edifice] stood another small tower which was also an idol-house or true hell, for one of its doors was in the shape of a terrible mouth, such as they paint to depict the jaws of hell. This mouth was open and contained great fangs to devour souls. [Note the universal notion of *devouring* souls.] Beside this door were groups of devils and the shapes of serpents, and a little way off was a place

14 14–16th C. Mesoamerican people of central Mexico

of sacrifice, all blood-stained and black with smoke. There were many great pots and jars and pitchers in this house, full of water. For it was here that they cooked the flesh of the wretched Indians who were sacrificed and eaten by the *papas*. Near this place of sacrifice there were many large knives and chopping-blocks like those on which men cut up meat in slaughter-houses.'

Perhaps, behind all these bloody sacrifices, lies some intimation that, man being what he eats, man can only be man if he eats man. It is argued in support of Christianity, that it consummates all that is true in the pagan myths and rituals, whereby they fall away, and that for the bloody sacrifice it has substituted the unbloody sacrifice. The Catholic Mass retains an element that would seem to belong to cannibalism. When Jesus told his followers that unless they eat his flesh and drink his blood they shall have no part in him, many fell away, presumably because they thought no true prophet would preach cannibalism. Jesus appeared to be out of his mind. But what he was actually saying is that you cannot participate in the life of God unless you palpably and with immediacy participate in the life of man. Further, Christ is the Son of Man. He is the representative man, which is why he incorporates all men in God. Hence partaking in his flesh and blood becomes a communion of all men with each other, since all men are sharing in the life of Man. Thus the feast at the altar becomes a *convivium*, a living together. There is no dead flesh on the altar because the life of God has overcome death. After this the eating of human flesh becomes a profanation, and the notion of cannibalism rightly causes revulsion. This has been brought about by a sublimation of cannibalism and not by its outright rejection. Man becoming what he eats becomes mankind, a citizen of the kingdom of God. By becoming what he eats he enters eternity.

Vegetarianism deserves more attention than it gets. In the only psychoanalytical case study which has come into my hands, the patient regarded vegetarianism as a defence against cannibalism. In eating meat we were not ennobling the flesh but dragging ourselves down to the bestial. If we eat beasts we become beasts. The patient regarded all carnivores as cannibals, so that eating animal food was intolerable. In love he had a great uneasiness about the contact of flesh with flesh. I do not know how universal the association of sex and vegetarianism may be. There does seem to me to be a connection between the Erewhonian[15] who surreptitiously ate steaks in a vegetarian society, and Ernest's[16] first encounter with a prostitute in *The Way of All Flesh*. Ernest's 'virtue' up to that time had been a mere puritanism of the body. How much vegetarianism is simply puritanism would be interesting to know. Mani's[17] father received a divine com-

15 Erewhon was a fictional country discovered by the protagonist in Samuel Butler's 1872 novel, *Erewhon*

16 Protagonist in Butler's semi-autobiographical anti-Victorian novel

17 (*c.* 210–276) Persian preacher and prophet and founder of Manichaeism

mand in a temple to abstain from flesh and women. Venturing on flesh in a vegetarian society appeared to Samuel Butler like venturing on a prostitute in Victorian[18] Christianity. Be this as it may, Christian man has been carnivorous man. Jesus was piscivorous even after the Resurrection, and did not become incarnate in a soya bean. Vegetarianism may become a religion, something having psychic and religious roots which go much deeper than the 'reasons' given for it by apologists. If we are not to have peace until vegetarians become kings, we might reflect that Hitler was a vegetarian.

Observe that I am not using 'vegetarian' as a swearword, but suggesting that it is an ambiguous phenomenon which, like food in general, is of more philosophical and psychological importance than is generally recognised. I own to having felt some annoyance recently on being asked by a Buddha addict whether I had arrived at vegetarianism yet, that is at her own high

18 Refers mainly to the reign of Queen Victoria which ran from 1837-1901, a period of industrial revolution, imperialism and sexual repression

level of insight. I suppose I should have replied with the words of a Zen master: If you see a Buddha, kill him. I feel the same about the Jesus freaks.

There must, in fact, be a very strong case for vegetarianism, if it can be accepted by half a billion Buddhists. Their motive is comprehensible and attractive: they have a reverence for life. They hold that there is no life without suffering, that suffering should arouse compassion, a compassion extending to all living beings, and forbidding us to kill. The Jains[19] also do not kill, the priest sweeping the ground before him to avoid treading on tiny forms of life. Because of this motive, vegetarianism is for some people a religion, sometimes a religion with all the rigidity and incapacity to compromise which characterises some forms of legalistic Christianity, or of Muslim and Jewish orthodoxy. In fact, they are bigots, willing to reprimand a God who had not yet arrived at vegetarianism, for saying 'Rise, Peter, kill and eat' (Acts 10:13).

---

19 An ancient philosophy and religion based upon the teaching of the prince Lord Mahavira (599–527 BC)

No doubt a religion of sarcophagy (flesh-eating) would also spawn some strange features.

I suspect that a certain amount of vegetarianism arises from squeamishness. I cannot bear to see a sheep's or an ox's throat cut, nor do I relish the duty of shooting domestic animals when they are old and ill. I could not look a beefsteak in the face after a tour of the abattoirs. This may go so far with some people that they go off meat altogether, and possibly find some religious sanction for an attitude which is in fact ethically indifferent. It may simply be the result of something which happened to you in the cowshed at the age of three. And in any event animal pain differs from human pain. Sorry, but it does! Most of our suffering is due to our ego's being in the forefront. *I* am hurt, *I* may be dying, *my* ear aches. We have a proprietorship in our suffering and are racked with fear because we can think, and because we are loath to lose this very power of thinking which enhances our pain. But the animal does not have that kind of ego, nor that kind of pain. The nemesis of treating animals as human is that we shall connect the eating of animal flesh with the taboo on cannibalism and become neurotic vegetarians. Further, once we treat animals as human, we shall in due course treat humans as animals. Behaviourism[20] and sentimentality go hand in hand. Then things will come full circle and we shall be defending cannibalism and making modest proposals for the eating of children. But there are more ways of devouring human beings than putting them in a pot. Scratch a sentimentalist and find a torturer, possibly disguised as a rich old lady with a Peke[21].

Some people do not have this kind of squeamishness. There are butchers like the celebrated butcher in Chuang-tzu who take an artist's pleasure in their job, and big game hunters who enjoy standing before the carcasses suspended in the shed after a day's hunt, and skinning and

20 An approach to psychology based on the theory that behaviour can be researched scientifically without reference to subjective mental states

21 Chinese breed of small short-legged dog

dismembering them. They may be men no less humane than you or I.

The fact is that we are situated in a world where life feeds on life, and to which life has been given so abundantly that there are lives to spare. Life is exuberant. And each of these lives is wonderful. One of the suasions against cannibalism is the immense distance between a man's life lived out, and a half-hour of the palate's delectation. However, this holds right down the scale, for every life is a miracle. One recalls what Sir Thomas Browne says about ants in *Religio Medici*:

'Ruder heads stand amazed at those prodigious pieces of Nature, Whales, Elephants, Dromidaries and Camels; these, I confess, are the Colossi and majestic pieces of her hand: but in these narrow engines there is more curious mathematics; and the civility of these little citizens more neatly sets forth the wisdom of their Maker.'

We have uncovered a good deal more of this mathematics since Browne's day. I find the ant's enginery as amazing as that of the starry heavens. Yet I do not hesitate to crush one when it tickles, as though the cessation of that tickle stood higher in the scale of being than that admirable little pismire[22]. It takes many small lives to make one big life. Life builds an ascending pyramid out of itself, and we had better look to the fact that it supports us.

The vegetable kingdom also comes into the picture. There, too, you have a miraculous frenzy of life, where mutual culling creates a harmony. Murdering a cabbage is not very different from crushing an ant. When you cut off its head it is dead and the vegetarian sits down to a platter of corpses. There is much more than foolery in Samuel Butler's account of the vegetarian episode in the history of Erewhon. The cabbage is of reality so compact that only God can know it through and through. And some of the most intelligent plants are carnivorous. If the lion is to lie down with

22 An ant, from the smell of formic acid that ants secrete

the lamb, let the vegetarian lie down with the cabbage.

Carnivorous plants seem to us to straddle the border between the animal and the vegetable, though we find nothing strange about herbivorous animals. The strangeness of the former has led story writers into fantasies about mobile plants which prowl about to look for flesh. It is in this twilit kingdom that beliefs about the mandrake[23] came into being. The mandrake is not a mythical beast but a well-known herb used medicinally. It sends forth a pleasant odour, but like poppy, it was not soporific enough for Lady Macbeth. It was credited with something human because its double root was taken to resemble a pair of human legs. Hence the mandrake was thought of as having a foot in both worlds. It was, as it were, a human vegetable.

By an amazing development of symbolism, the mandragora or mandrake came to indicate salvation. Since it has a leg in both the animal and vegetable worlds, it brings the vegetarian and the

23 Plant family belonging to the nightshades, long used in magic, believed to shriek in pain when pulled from the ground

sarcophagus together. It shrieks when lifted, and, according to the beliefs of the Hellenic world, had to be lifted at night, the digger facing the West and attaching the mandrake by a string to a black dog which would give the final jerk — and then perish!

In the Middle Ages, in the *Trudperter Hohelied*[24] — on which Hugo Rahner comments in his *Greek Myths and Christian Mystery* — the symbolism takes on this final form: 'In this Christ himself appears as the divine rhizotomist[25] who lifts the screaming mandrake, which is mankind, out of the earth, so that he may endow it with the power of blossoming everlastingly, and give it an undying fragrance. This he does by the power of his incarnation through which he descended into the dark kingdom in which our human roots are embedded. Then, by an extraordinary boldness of metaphor Christ himself is, at the final coming, conceived as the mandrake who, by the crying out of

24 Commentary on the biblical high song

25 Rhizotomy is the surgical severance of spinal nerve roots to relieve pain or hypertension

its mighty voice, becomes a dispenser of everlasting life and death.'

Not the vegetarian then, but the eater of the mandrake which is the saving flesh of God, is fit for a kingdom in which man shall be fully human. The animal and the vegetable are reconciled in one life which 'plays in ten thousand places.'

Think on this when next you marry meat and vegetables in a stew. It is a mystical marriage, a reconciliation. The vegetarian lies down with the sarcophagus. Animal and vegetable come together in an oblation which the two and seventy shrieking sects confute. The vegetation cults and the bloody sacrifices are sublated in the corn and wine which become flesh and blood. The root, which screams when it is lifted from the tomb, sings the song of songs at Easter, for now the mandrake gives forth a pleasant odour.

I have spoken about those who are vegetarians by conviction. However, those who are vegetarians of necessity are quite another matter. Usually it is the price of meat which creates them — lamb chops today cost just fifty times what they cost when I was a boy. Lamb addicts, of which I am one, have often to look elsewhere for a full belly. For them let me suggest a few vegetarian dishes. They are easier to provide for than vegetarians of the pure observance because they do not boggle at a stock cube or strip of bacon or the gravy from yesterday's roast to add interest to the concoction. Not that vegetables can't stand alone, as evidenced in many Chinese stir-fries. The strict vegetarian, who makes lentils into steak, may want to make his signature look like yours — he is forging or faking.

While on the general subject of vege-tarianism, I might mention that yesterday somebody brought me a copy of a Zen cookery book which is one of the most un-Zennish things I have ever laid eyes on. Even before reading further than the cover, I found that it set out to divulge the secret of longevity and rejuvenation. But what one ought to learn from Zen is to take a long life or a short life with equal composure. Proceeding further, I found

myself confronted with a system no different from any Western system of organised
prejudices. One has to spend this long life
doing obeisance to a dish of brown rice.
Food is divided into yin food and yang
food, very much like our medieval system
of cold and hot humours, with brown rice
as a panacea or *remedium universale*. On
my shelves there is a medical textbook of
the 18th century which professes to have the
secret of two sovereign remedies, a Solar
Tincture for all ills of men (yang), and a
Lunar Tincture for all ills of women (yin).
The fact that the book under discussion has
a mystique of vitamins adds nothing new
to the underlying attitudes. It is just a sort
of self-styled Zen domestic science manual,
and nowhere did I find an attempt to spell
out the really profound dictum: Zen is to
eat when you are hungry and drink when
you are thirsty.

I communicate this gem to you: 'A man
who eats only pork comes to resemble
a pig and to behave like a pig in any
circumstances. A meat eater is not as quiet
as a vegetable eater. The meat eater gets

angry easily. He is explosive, while the vegetable eater lives in the diurnal tranquillity of a flower, opening to light, then closing with the day's end.' *Ecce flos!* Also, *das Schwein ist was es isst* (the pig is what it eats). A pig will make a pig of itself eating rice.

A bad prospect for the Chinese who are great eaters of pork! In fact, a Chinese girl is coming to us this evening to make the traditional sweet-and-sour pork. And lo! The poor Inuit! Not for him now shuts the crimson petal, now the white. If I do not regard, with tranquillity, the spiritual condition of the Inuit, his stomach full of seal meat and blubber, it must be because I ate sausage last night. I may say that potatoes, tomatoes and egg-plants are tranquilly thrown into the outer darkness where there is wailing and gnashing of teeth. Now you know how the Irish got to be like that.

Zen may be idiosyncratic, but one of its idiosyncrasies is that it doesn't encourage one to impose one's idiosyncrasies on others. Further, where the comic spirit is absent, there is no Zen. Laughter is the most important of all the spices. I have found our author laughing just about as loudly as a potato flower closing up for the night. Or perhaps it doesn't close up!

While in this yangish mood — it is just the time of morning when I open up to the light — I must aver that I have received much more rudeness from vegetarians than from sarcophagi. My shooting and drinking friends are easy, because they don't make a religion of the whole business. It takes a religion to create real bad manners because it can be so unaccommodating. I recall my annoyance one evening — must have been eating beef — when I was singled out by a very eminent visiting imam, part of whose invited and captive audience I was, to put up with an attack on existentialism in which he knew I was interested and of which he knew nothing. But when Catholics were bound by the rule of abstinence from meat on Fridays, it was pretty generally recognised that on some special occasions, and when one was the guest of poor people, or of those who knew nothing of Catholicism, charity and good manners bade one eat what was offered.

If you want an absolute rule, try this one: Charity and courtesy outweigh any dogma. Don't swap God for a bowl of rice, or friendship for a soya bean, no matter how long you may live.

However, let us get back to those who are in the main vegetarians for the scientifically foolproof reason that they can't get a pig into their purses. It is a matter of financial capacity much more certain than the hypothesis that rice is the master food.

Here is a red cabbage pie which requires very little animal matter and can feed a large family very economically. In a large, heavy pot put a layer of finely sliced red cabbage, then a layer of sliced onions and then a layer of sliced cooking apples (cabbage has an affinity for apples). Repeat the layers. Lay a few rashers of bacon on top, warding off Circe[26], if you wish, by

26 Also Kirke or Aeaea, Greek mythological enchantress who turned the companions of Odysseus into swine; her spells could be counteracted by the use of the magic herb, moly

111

spells or by holding up a moly plant. Pour over all this a tumbler of vinegar and red wine, sweetened with brown sugar or honey, and half a cup of oil. Insert a few cloves and bake. You can play variations of this theme by using layers of good and heavy, solid pumpkin, with salt and pepper, of course.

If you want this to be really filling, add dumplings. Dumplings ought to be interesting in themselves, and have their flavour and character. My own very simple procedure is to put flour in a bowl with baking powder, salt, pepper, and turmeric, or garam masala (ground mixed spice), or ground meat, or celery or what have you. Make a stiff dough with a little milk, roll into fairish-sized marbles and drop into the boiling soup.

X

The Sea for Dinner

Putting it that way, and remembering what I have said about the divinity of food, one can see that a case can also be made out for the divinity of water. This has already been done in such old Upanishads as the Brihadaranyaka and Chandogya: 'In the beginning the world was just water.' 'It is pure water solidified that is this earth, that is the atmosphere, that is the sky, that is gods and men, beasts and birds, grass and trees, animals together with worms, flies and ants. All these are just water solidified. Reverence water.' That is as much as Epicurus[1] managed to do with his atoms, which he did *not* ask us to reverence. That is why, contrary to popular belief, he recommended a rather poor table. He could not turn his bread and water into flesh and the wine into blood.

There is nothing in modern biological

---

1 (341–270 BC) Ancient Greek philosopher, founder of Epicureanism, devoted to the pursuit of sensual pleasure

science to kill the notion of the watery deeps as the Great Mother. We are told that we crawled out of the sea when its temperature and salinity were that of our blood. In fact, we are said to go back to primal green smears of algae in the intertidal zone, some of which crept forwards and some backwards to become the marine and terrestrial animal and vegetable kingdoms. You may not like having your descent traced from an anthropoid, but how about putting a bit of primitive and ambiguous seaweed at the top of the family tree? I find it rather consoling, since only love could have made so good a job out of such unpromising material. I cannot understand why some Bible Christians make no fuss about having originated from dust, but get up on their hind legs when they are said to have descended from so lovingly constructed a job as an anthropoid who got up on *his* hind legs. Perhaps if the anthropoid could have foreseen some of his descendants, *he* would have taken a poor view of evolutionary theory.

But having argued the divinity of food, which is mostly water anyhow, I don't think I'll go further and argue the divinity of water as well. Merely as the place of origin of seafoods, it has more than a fair claim to divinity; and in any event we treat it as scurvily as though it were God incarnate. It is the scapegoat that has to carry our sewage. If we no longer hear old Triton blow his wreathed horn, it may be that he can't get through the slick, or has died of mercury poisoning. Perhaps he has been dredged up by a trawler and put in an anti-god museum. The state of the seas and rivers shows how far we have strayed from the injunction: Reverence water. *Saevis tranquillus in undis* — for the waves are less savage than the purulent muck we pour into them. That's no way to treat your mother! Let us remember that when we eat, we eat the sea, for even bread's moisture comes from the sea's vapours. It is as well to recollect that the sea is not some abstract water which has in it, distinct from itself, salt and fish and shells and seaweed. The sea is water and fish, just as the wind is not something apart from the blown tree, but is the tree, as it is a number of things which it is only supposed to do. The wind in the willows and the bats in the belfry are unitary phenomena. We are as much nature as our faces and mouths, which have to speak for her.

> And what is Earth's eye, tongue, or heart
>   else, where
> Else, but in dear and dogged man?
>   — Ah, the heir
> To his own selfbent so bound, so tied
>   to his turn,
>
> To thriftless reave both our rich round
>   world bare
> And none reek of world after, this bids wear
> Earth brows of such care, care and
>   dear concern.
>
> (Hopkins[2])

Instead of theologising on the sea, I propose rather to make a small anthology of literature on the sea, the motivation

---

2   From 'Ribblesdale' by Gerard Manley Hopkins

of which is as follows: Eating is not only a physical process; it is also a spiritual process. Your food could not enter your mouth, did it not first enter your mind. You are what you eat, but you also eat what you are. You pour a spiritual sauce on what enters your mouth, like an act of sex which is clothed with imagination. Bread — just think of it, what a beautiful word! You think of Ruth[3] standing in tears amid the alien corn, or of the corn which is orient and immortal wheat, which never should be reaped nor was ever sown. *Bread* — in that *r* you break it, in that *d* you descend into the earth like the dead who are sown in corruption. You clothe what you eat with memory, philosophy, imagination and experience.

We all have our store of spiritual sources. Seafood we must invest with the sea, for it *is* the sea, and what is said about the sea is said about it. And how much has been said! I stand dumbfounded before such evocations. Let me set down

3 Old Testament character, one of only two women to have a book of the Bible named after them, great-grandmother of David and ancestress of Jesus

some that happen to occur to me. Eating fish is not just eating fish! It is having the sea for dinner, and your sea is all that has been written and sung about it. England produced Shakespeare[4], and in thanks Shakespeare produced England. In the same way Homer[5] and Melville and a thousand others produced the sea. They are the magic casements from which we see its perilous foam. Nothing is really itself until it enters the world through the doors of poetry. The fathers of the Church declared that the world is the *poiesis*, the making, of God, for a poet is a maker, and therefore the Creator is *the* Poet. There is a very real sense in which Shakespeare created the English spring when he wrote:

When daisies pied and violets blue
And lady-smocks all silver-white
And cuckoo-buds of yellow hue
Do paint the meadows with delight.

4 William Shakespeare (1564–1616), English poet and playwright, considered to be one of the greatest writers
5 Legendary 9th C. BC Greek epic poet, reputed author of the *Iliad* and *Odyssey*

It is the poets who make the real world which lives beneath the phantasmagoria of politicians. England will last, not for as long as there is a Labour Party, but for as long as there is a Shakespeare. Wordsworth[6] did not invoke Cromwell[7], but Milton[8].

Politics is not patriotism — it uses a simulacrum of the latter for its own purposes.

To come now to the Ocean and the sea-foods which are the Ocean, in the sense in which the bending tree is the wind, I shall do no more in this chapter than recall some of the verses which have made the sea real for me. Other people will recall others — the sea is large. The *Odyssey* remains the best sauce when dining on the sea. The sea has a luminous quality, for Ocean is a great god.

That dolphin-torn, that gong-tormented sea.

(Yeats[9])

6 William Wordsworth (1770–1850), major English poet

7 Oliver Cromwell (1599–1658), English military leader and politician

8 John Milton (1608–1674), English poet, most famous for *Paradise Lost*

9 From 'Byzantium' by William Butler Yeats (1865–1939)

The dragon-green, the luminous, the dark,
the serpent-haunted sea.

(Flecker[10])

In Xanadu did Kubla Khan
A stately pleasure-dome decree;
Where Alph, the sacred river, ran
Through caverns measureless to man
Down to a sunless sea.

(Coleridge[11])

The image of the river's plunging into tumult in the sunless sea raises those goose pimples which, Plato says, mark where the feathers grew when we flew in the heaven of Beauty before our fall into a corruptible body. Homer's 'wine-dark sea' also has this luminous quality, for the sea in Homer is a person. We feel the eternity of this sea again in Tennyson's[12] 'Ulysses', which evokes so many moods of the sea:

Through scudding drifts the rainy Hyades
Vext the dim sea . . .

10 From 'The Gates of Damascus' by James Elroy Flecker (1884–1915)

11 From 'Kubla Khan' by Samuel Taylor Coleridge (1772–1834)

12 Alfred Tennyson (1809–1892), English poet laureate

. . . for my purpose holds
To sail beyond the sunset, and the baths
Of all the western stars, until I die.

But there are also the homely stars made
by men:

The lights begin to twinkle from the rocks:
The long day wanes: the slow moon climbs:
   the deep
Moans round with many voices.

The Afrikaner[13] is not primarily a
seaman. His great voyages have been over
land. He, too, looked for a Paradise by
following the setting sun and, like so many
who take up this quest, left his bones in the
Thirstland. To leave your ribs eroded by
the sand dunes, or lie, tugged by the rise
and fall of the sea swell, is perhaps not so
very different. In any event, the magic of
strange landfalls is still with us, brought to
us down the ages from the early navigators
who live on in our poets, navigators in

13 Afrikaans-speaking descendent of Dutch settlers who
colonised southern Africa from 1652

their own right.

Such patriotism is worth a million automatic rifles, but the cost is greater: You have to give up your ego. No wonder it is not provided for in the Budget!

Not only poetry but cooking, too, can be epic. Ho Chi Minh[14], who beat the Americans in Vietnam, was once Escoffier's[15] pastry cook, a good training for an epic achievement. So I will pause to tell you how he dealt with the abalone wrenched from among the stonefish and green-black crawfish. *Pietas*[16] will not bar me from some modifications of my own, but in principle I learnt from him how not to botch up the best of all seafoods. You should use live abalone. Get them out of the shell by twisting a broad screwdriver under the attachment. In my opinion all the scraping and scouring that is supposed to follow is unnecessary. Had we but life enough and time! Scrub off the sand and

14 (1890–1969) Vietnamese revolutionary and statesman, President of North Vietnam 1954–1969

15 Georges Auguste Escoffier (1846–1935), French chef, restaurateur and culinary writer

16 Respected ancestor or forerunner

slime with a scrubbing brush in diluted vinegar. Do not cut off the fringe, which is delicious. Divide the shellfish in two horizontally — or cut fingers, if you wish — wrap the pieces in a rag and pound them gently. Do not hammer the hell out of them, but just tap them a bit until they relax. Dry them very thoroughly and heat copious butter in a heavy pot. *Don't* put the flesh in water or wine, but drop it straight into the sizzling butter. Ten minutes of cooking, at most, should suffice. Whip out the pieces as soon as a fork slides easily through them, and keep them in a warm dish. Mix milk and cornflour, and lemon juice into the remaining butter. Dash with old brandy and pour over the abalone, with grated nutmeg and black pepper. You can taste for salt, though it should be salt enough, and garnish with parsley if you like. Serve with rice or floury potatoes, with as much salad and white wine as you think fit.

To get the best enjoyment from your seafood you should fetch it in yourself. Perhaps you have got up, just before daybreak — for fish bite best in the twilight — and tramped barefoot between the water's edge and the great mounds of uprooted kelp hopping with sandfleas, past the wreckage cast up by the sea: oaken boards, fish baskets, the glassy globes of floats, cordage, tangles of nylon fishing line, sharks' eggs and jellyfish, the jetsam your subconscious casts up in your dreams. Your wet shorts chafe your thighs, and your rod feels like a pole as you look for some wild gully where bubble is a world, and where you hope to feel the fast pluck of a galjoen. Or you have been breaking your back spinning into the sunrise at Rooikranz[17]. You are dead tired, perhaps you have caught a noble yellowtail[18] or two, and you lie back drinking in the growing warmth and perhaps remembering the majesty of Lucretius'[19] aubade[20]:

17 Literally 'red cliff,' situated near the tip of the Cape Peninsular near Cape Town, considered one of the world's best rock fishing spots

18 Cape or California yellowtail, *Seriola lalandi*, with firm white flesh when cooked

19 Titus Lucretius Carus (99–55 BC), Roman poet and philosopher

20 Poem or piece of music accompanying or evoking daybreak

Look where another of our Gods, the Sun,
Apollo, Helios, or of older use
All-seeing Hyperion . . .
King of the East although he seem and girt
With song and flame and fragrance,
    slowly lifts
His golden feet on those empurpled stairs
That climb into the windy halls of heaven.

                   (Tennyson)

The windy halls — a sublime touch, for there must be a bit of a south-easterly to put silver caps on the wine-dark sea; and in the swirls against the rock face, 'Lithe turning of water, sinews of Poseidon', the water 'colour of grape's pulp' (Pound[21]).

And so one could go on, the fair breeze blowing, the *Spray* with a bone in her teeth, to the days when:

The air was calm, and on the level brine
Sleek Panope with all her sisters played.

                    (Milton)

---

21 Ezra Weston Loomis Pound (1885–1972), American expatriate, poet, musician and critic

I cannot gather the sea in a cup, nor draw out Leviathan with a hook.

Rax me my cloak! I'll down the Quay
And see him come ashore
(from *Minstrelsy of Scotland*).

The Ancient Mariner[22];
Joshua Slocum[23] from the *Spray*;
Heyerdahl[24] from *Kon-Tiki*;
Darwin[25] from the *Beagle*;
Melville from the *Pequod*;
Bullen[26] from the *Cachalot*.

Magellan, Drake, Cook, Nansen and Conrad, Odysseus and Herodotus, the old Phoenicians[27] who first sailed round the Cape. You can have them all for dinner.

22 'Rime of the Ancient Mariner,' S. T. Coleridge poem written 1778–1779

23 (1844–1909) Canadian seaman and adventurer, the first person to sail single-handedly around the world

24 Thor Heyerdahl (1914–2002), Norwegian marine biologist and anthropologist, famous for his 1947 expedition

25 Charles Robert Darwin (1809–1882), English naturalist and originator of the theory of evolution through natural selection

26 Frank T. Bullen, author of *The Cruise of the Cachalot* (*c.* 1899)

27 All famous explorers and adventurers

But there is also the sea of Stevenson's Gordon Darnaway[28]:

'There's devils in the deep sea would yoke on a communicant! Eh, sirs, if ye had gone doon wi' the puir lads in the Christ — Anna, ye would ken by now the mercy o' the seas. If ye had sailed it for as long as me, ye would hate the thocht of it as I do. If ye had but used the een God gave ye, ye would hae learned the wickedness o' that fause, saut, cauld, bullering creature, and of a' thats' in it by the Lord's permission: Labsters and partans, an' sic-like, howking in the deid; muckle, gutsy, blawing whales; an' fish — the hale clan o' them — cauld wamed, blind — ee'd uncanny ferlies — Oh sirs, the horror, the horror o' the sea!'

I prefer Rachel Carson[29]. She did not, like Darnaway, murder the sea, but

---

28 Character in Robert Louis Balfour Stevenson's *The Merry Men*

29 (1907–1964) US zoologist and biologist whose landmark book, *Silent Spring*, is credited with launching the global environmental movement

like Cousteau[30], tried to save its life. Xenophon's[31] men made history when they cried 'Thalassa, thalassa!' (the sea, the sea).' But the sea's future history depends on us, and we have our Salamis[32] to win over the corruptors of nature.

But before we ruin the sea, which is our mother, before it is poisoned by the red tides caused by the greed of over-fishing, gather some black mussels far from a sewage outlet into this beshitted ocean, and let me suggest how you may cook them. Take eighty to a hundred black mussels and put them in a large pot with celery, parsley, leeks and a cup of white wine. Shaking occasionally, bring them to the boil and remove from the fire as soon as they gape, which is very soon indeed. Shell the mussels and strain the liquid through muslin. Overcooking is fatal.

Fry six shelled prawns in four

30 Jacques-Yves Cousteau (1910–1997), French naval officer, explorer, ecologist and researcher

31 (427–355 BC) Greek soldier, historian and student of Socrates

32 Great naval battle between the Greek city-states and Persia in 480 BC

tablespoons of butter with crushed garlic *q.s.*[33] Then add the mussel juice and mix in a carton of sour cream and a pinch of red pepper.

If you want to eat it as soup, don't thicken it. If you want to pour it over rice, thicken with cornflour. Use nutmeg and parsley if you like, but no salt.

33 *Quantum sufficit,* as much as is sufficient

XI

Herbs and Spices

Herbs and spices do for your dishes what grace does for your actions — they give them zest and an inner meaning. The graceless life is the life which has lost its savour. Rue is called the herb of grace. When you have expelled the witches with it, use the expressed juice mixed with honey for your cough.

Herb gardens once served two purposes, but that was before we preferred a dollar's worth of pills to a dollar's worth of herbs. Herb gardens were once our medicine chests and my grandmother had a witchdoctor's skill in using them. We once saved a woman's leg, which the surgeon wished to amputate, by washing it with a decoction of wild salvia. However, the medicinal properties of herbs are not relevant here, except that we should remember how closely related the kitchen and the dispensary are. One eats one's way to health. We have a symbol of this relationship in our kitchen: a large wooden-handled carbon-steel spatula, used by old Mr Ross of Kloof Street seventy years ago in his pharmacy. Keats's 'lucent syrops, tinct with cinnamon'[1] is very like some of old Sir Thomas Browne's prescriptions.

I own to a belief that a human body delicately suffused with fragrances is healthier than one which is not, a belief I share with Sir Thomas. I take the following from a letter to his son, Dr Edward Browne (12 September 1680): 'I read over Apitius *de re culinaria* and also Platina, where there is mention of many odde pickles, in many whereof was cummin seed of an ungratefull tast. I contrived a pickle out of oysters, anchovies, pickled cowcumbers, onyons, Rhenish wine, etc. which I caused your mother to make, and I gave it to a patient whose weake and vomiting stomack was helped thereby . . . It pleased us so well that I called it *muria regalis*.'

Pleasant for a doctor to be able to have his prescriptions for dinner. I wonder when last that happened.

1   From 'The Eve of St Agnes' by John Keats (1795–1821)

Books on pharmacy were actually Herbals. I have to hand an English version of M. Pomet's[2] *Complete History of Drugs: A Work of Very Great Use and Curiosity*, from which I take this paragraph at random: 'Citron-peels come also to us from Spain and Portugal; those which look fresh and of lively yellow colours, and that have a fragrant smell, are best; if the colour and the smell be decay'd they are not of much value. They are Cephalick, neurotick, stomackick, cardiack, hysterick, and alexipharmick, good against all cold and moist Diseases of the Head and Nerves, Bitings of Serpents and mad dogs, and all sorts of malign and pestilential Diseases; measles, small-pox, plague, surfeits, etc.' — which gives us wide scope to speculate on what Dr Johnson did with the orange peels remaining after punch had been brewed, something which, smiling mysteriously, he would never divulge.

Having opened Pomet, let me give you one more extract just for the fun of it:

2 Pierre Pomet (1658–1699), French storekeeper and chief druggist to King Louis XIV

'Oh Cochinille. The Cochinille, called *Mestick*, is the seed of a plant about two or three feet high, adorned with leaves two fingers thick, of a beautiful green, and very prickly; among which grow Husks in form of a Heart, of a green, tending to a yellow colour; in which are enclosed a quantity of small seeds of the size of a great Pins-head, in shape sometimes flat, sometimes triangular, but always rough, of a greyish silver colour to the Eye, and as red as Blood within. The Plant which bears them is called *Opuntium*.'

However, the great Plumier[3] makes things somewhat clearer being the first who spoke 'with any Degree of Propriety of this Drug: for his comparing it to a Bug, is much more just, than the later opinion of making it a kind of Lady Cow to which it has not the least resemblance.' Even tobacco gets a kind word: 'They make, by Distillation of Tobacco with Flegm of Vitriol, a Liquor that is emetic, or very

3   Charles Plumier (1646–1704), French botanist and member of the Order of the Minims

vomitive, and proper to cure itch and scabs.'

A friend of mine could have contributed to this Herbal when, after having been made free of somebody's herb garden, he found he was cooking with 'grass.' He said it was not disagreeable.

There is no more profitable way of using limited garden space than by planting herbs. Indeed, one can do very well with troughs placed on a sunny balcony or at the kitchen door. Collectors of herbs are apt to be like young stamp collectors — they want as many kinds as possible. It is a pleasant hobby and there are quite a number of little handbooks on the culture and use of herbs, so I need not say much about this. The best way to get stocks is from friends — herbs are apt to multiply, and the cook-gardener likes to dispense his savours. Packets of mixed seeds can give good results, or young plants can be obtained from a nursery. From the point of view of mere utility it is better to have a good supply of a few sorts than too little of many sorts. Every cook will make his own selection, though there are some which are essential. I shall list and annotate some of those at present in our own garden.

Chives are easily grown and prolific. They flower and seed freely.

Shallots have much the same use as chives, but are best grown from bulbs, which subdivide and multiply very freely. One can either crop the shoots or break away a few bulbs.

Parsley is essential and is grown from seed.

Coriander is usually used as dried seed, but it should be grown and used like parsley. It has an excellent and delicate flavour. Green coriander is essential to curry.

Basil is an annual grown from seed, though cuttings root quickly in a tumbler of water. It is indeed a *basileus*, a king of herbs, wonderful in most salads. It was created to consort with tomato in salads.

Lovage is a powerful and assertive herb, somewhat reminiscent of celery. It has real character and is worth experimenting with.

Sage is a hardy perennial. Sage and onions.

Origanum is more difficult to control than to grow. Try to get a rooted runner from a friend. It is indispensable for Mediterranean cooking.

Thyme is delicious and versatile. Stews and meats. Beef olives are not beef olives without it.

All the above can be accommodated in pots or troughs. Give them good soil and water them occasionally with a plant food, especially where the soil in troughs is in danger of leaching out.

Rosemary often grows into a bush five feet in diameter and is easily started in autumn from slips about fifteen centimetres long. Necessary in spaghetti sauces and with beef, and used in marinating beef and game.

Bay or *laurel*. We happen to have a bush and find it useful in curries. But you can dispense with it if there is a pittosporum tree in your neighbourhood; in any event, it remains potent when dry. Lemon leaves are also a good substitute.

Ginger. Green ginger has such a delicious tang that it is worthwhile securing a supply. What you use is the rhizome, but the plant is handsome, rather like a small canna, with a brilliant scarlet or pale yellow bloom.

Fennel is quite common and often there for the gathering. The seed is used in many dishes such as biryani and the chopped foliage in salads and marinades, and as garnishing for fish. It reaches a height of about two metres and seeds freely. Tea from fennel seed was said to make you 'gaunt and lank.'

Chillies are easily grown, but we usually just buy a handful and pickle them in vinegar and brine for use when wanted, which, with my Oriental palate, is fairly often. To use them without disaster needs prudence. Remember, it is the seeds that have the bite. When in doubt, substitute sweet peppers.

Mint. Well, of course. There are about forty varieties.

We have, also, balm, savory, tarragon and hyssop.

In the Cape Peninsula there are two *Umbelliferae*[4] worthy of mention. The first is a wild celery which grows where bits of marshy ground abut on the sea. It is incomparably superior to any cultivated celery. The other is the blister bush, well cursed by all mountaineers because it is deserving of its name. I have heard an infusion of it recommended for dropsy[5]. It has a powerful odour which makes it attractive to the caterpillar of the Christmas butterfly, which likes those strong oils found also in lemon leaves and rue. I have not experimented with this. In fact, the idea of doing so has only just struck me, and I pass the idea on. Perhaps one could try it in bobotie[6]. It is also called *wilde seldery* or wild celery.

You need not reserve a special part of your garden for herbs. By and large they are beautiful in their own right and can

4 Also call *Apiaceae*, large plant family including parsley, carrots and other relatives

5 Also oedema, a swelling of any organ or tissue due to accumulation of excess fluid

6 S. African dish of Malaysian origin, spiced minced meat baked with a custard topping

be mixed with other flowering plants in a herbaceous border. 'Blue flowering borage, the Aleppo sort' deserves better than to be tucked away in a kitchen garden. Kitchen herbs are also flowering plants. A row of chives in flower is most attractive, and the blue-green foliage of rue is very pleasing. To do them justice in a herbaceous border, kitchen herbs must be planted in some quantity, but in actual fact you can hardly have too many. It is lovely to walk in the garden when your herbs have been warmed by the sun, or distilled by the moon. They can be made into decorative arrangements for the house, when they will also make their presence smelt.

Herbs and spices are not brittle, dry stuff in bottles. Further, they do not merely accompany or garnish spring and summer; they *are* spring and summer. Spring is not a date in a calendar. It is a rising tide of vegetation. Certain butterflies do not appear on, say, the fifteenth of September. They, and the flowers they seek, and the sky against which we see them, *are* the fifteenth of September. In the same way the wind and the swaying willow are not two 'things'; the wind *is* the swaying willow. We think that the wind does something to the willow, forgetting what the willow does to the wind. It makes it actual. Time and space, in reality, apprehended without our abstractions, are a togetherness and flow of happenings. They are a 'mutual arising.' Real space is a conjunction of places. Time *is* the flowing of events into amaryllis lilies and black butterflies. The lilies do something to time: They fade and that is what makes time something that passes. We think: Spring *has* herbs, we *have* time to look at them, we *have* bodies with which to experience the fragrance. Thus does our possessiveness disembowel reality. It is the separated ego which *has*. But in fact spring *is* herbs, I *am* a filament of time, we *are* our bodies as seen from within and not as so many ounces of matter.

Arise, my darling,
my lovely one, and come with me.
See! The winter is past;
the rains are over and gone.

Flowers appear on the earth;
the season of glad songs has come,
the cooing of the turtle-dove is heard in our
     land.
The fig tree is forming its first figs
and the blossoming vines spread their
     fragrance.

                    (Song of Solomon 2: 10-13)

That is spring. It is not a date. We, in saying this, are spring, and from what we are in the centre comes the vesture of eternity, which clothes the transient flowers and doves and figs.

There are two condiments, falling somewhere between herbs and spices, which I ought to mention. The first is garlic. When one buys garlic in my part of the world one is usually offered a large white bulb. This is not good garlic. In fact, we call it *beesknoffel*, cattle garlic. The pinkish, smaller type is very much better. In a cookbook which sells like hot cakes I find the following: 'As garlic is very strong, only minute amounts should be used . . . half a small clove is plenty to flavour a soup or stew for four people.' Thus the whole ear of Denmark is corrupt. Write upon you palate: Garlic is good, lots of garlic is better.

By way of impressing this on you, I give you a recipe, requiring twenty-five large cloves of garlic, which I made successfully for my somewhat spiky family. Nobody smelt any the worse for it. It is a spicy seafood dish.

Start off by slicing your garlic together with a large onion. Put them in a pan with an adequacy of oil and braise until soft. This, by the way, works much better if you add a tablespoon of water to the oil. Lift them out with one of those spoons with holes in it. Into the oily pan put a chopped-up chilli and, if you like, a small cube of *trasi*[7], four skinned tomatoes, a large pinch of turmeric, six mashed black olives and salt. Then put in two good cups of prawns, or well-soaked dried shrimps, fuse them with the other stuff, mix in your garlic and onion, and simmer *q.s.*

Let me tell you how to store garlic. Buy it when it is cheapest and break the bulb

7   Dried shrimp paste

into cloves. Put these in a small basin and drench them with boiling water, which makes them very easy to husk. Put them in a jar and cover them with oil, where they will last indefinitely. You can pour off a little of the oil now and then for a salad dressing, topping up with fresh oil.

I suggest a wide use of olives. Olives being expensive, I shall tell you how to pickle your own ripe olives — nice soft odoriferous black olives for cooking and not the green pebbles you get at sherry parties.

Use olives which are black and ripe, but firm, and cut a longitudinal slit in each. Put them in a basin of water, which should be changed twice a day for three weeks. Then prepare a brine, using one cup of coarse salt to five litres of water, and let the olives lie in this for a week. Pour off the brine and pour on vinegar, in which you leave the olives for approximately five hours. Drain off the vinegar, which you can keep for cooking, and mix more brine. Bottle the olives in the brine, putting in the bottom of each jar two slices of lemon and a bay-leaf. Top the jars with a layer of oil to seal them. You can put your olives in pure cooking oil, which you can use afterwards as olive oil.

Talking of olives, here is a good recipe for beef olives. Thin tenderised steak should be used, cut into eight-centimetre squares. Prepare chopped herbs, which must include thyme and rosemary, and mix them with mashed garlic and olives and salt and pepper. Take flour and make a stiff dough which you may spice, for instance, with mace, and cut it into thin three-inch strips. Take fat, smoked pork and cut it into similar strips. Put dough, pork and herbs on your squares of beef. Roll them up and secure with toothpicks. Put some oil in a heavy pot and braise your meat *q.s.* You should put a few olives and shallots in the pot.

I was shown a Victorian cookery book recently which gave the estimated prices of the dishes described. What stability, when prices could be relied on to stay put between the writing and proofreading stages! Beef olives for a festive dinner party of six cost three shillings and four pence.

Then there is the story of the Irish country cousin who was taken to a cocktail party by a city friend. He was offered, and tried, some black olives. 'Say, Mike,' he whispers to his friend, 'somebody has pissed on the prunes!'

Having dealt with the 'isness' of herbs and olives, we can go on to spices, a subject so often dealt with that I need not merely be repetitive here.

I start with the suggestion that you read the Song of Solomon, all of it and not just this bit:

Your shoots form an orchard of
    pomegranates,
the rarest essences are yours:
nard and saffron,
calamus and cinnamon,
with all the incense-bearing trees,
myrrh and aloes,
with the subtlest odours.
Fountain that makes the gardens fertile,
well of living water,
streaming down from Lebanon.

(4:13-15)

Do this as a meditation before starting to cook, and recipes will arise spontaneously.

Cape cooks are spice conscious because Cape Town came into being as a halfway-house between Holland or the Netherlands and the Spice Islands. But we need have no nostalgia about the demise of the Dutch East India Company[8]. Many of its directors, the Heren Sewentien (Lords Seventeen) are doubtless in hell. One of my own ancestors, a governor of Ceylon (now Sri Lanka), was assassinated and, to judge by his portrait, very appropriately too.

It takes a long time to use any spice properly. It needs a well-trained palatal imagination. Simple tools are sometimes not quite as easy to use as they at first appear to be. I find that everybody thinks he can use an axe, yet to judge by the broken hafts and chipped edges of my axes, hardly anybody can. I can tell you to put green ginger into fig jam, and not cloves or nutmeg, but it would be better if you worked it out for yourself. Failures are

8 VOC in Dutch, established in 1602, the first multinational company and the first company to issue stock

sometimes better cooking ventures than 'successes.' The pleasure of growing is more important than that of showmanship.

I shall simply list what I find on our shelves at the moment of writing:

Black, white and lemon peppers. Also whole
    black peppers and allspice.
Nutmeg, cloves, cinnamon,
fenugreek *(methi)*, cumin *(gira)*, fennel seed,
sesame-seed and black Kalonji[9],
ground ginger, root ginger, and
    NB turmeric,
coriander, whole and ground, paprika,
two garam masalas,
asafoetida[10] *(duiwelsdrek* or devil's shit).

There are aromatic flavouring salts which, if used too prodigally, will ruin your cooking. Mixed spices for steaks, chops, barbecues, etc., are despised by

---

9 *Nigella sativa*, an annual flowering plant native to southwest Asia with a pungent bitter taste, aka fennel flower, black caraway, black cumin, nutmeg flower, Roman coriander, nigella or black seeds

10 *Ferula asafoetida*, a resin gum which comes from the dried sap of the wild fennel, aka *hing* in many of the northern Indian languages

those who don't want even their privacies mass-produced. You may choose to grind your own garam masala. If you want something special for your barbecues, strew fresh rosemary on the coals.

While we are stock-taking, let's run over the bottles:

Soy sauce (we're out of oyster sauce).
Several vinegars, including wine and cider vinegars, and sherry, in which a few chillies have been steeped, for soups.
Olive oil and sunflower oil (we should have sesame oil).
Wine, especially dry red.

A salad dressing can be made like this: Mince garlic, olives, and shallots; add chopped chives. Beat up the yolk of an egg, add a dessert-spoon of cornflour, pepper and salt, and brown sugar with some diluted vinegar, bring to the boil, then add your herbs and olive oil to taste.

It is both salubrious and conducive to salvation to memorise this:

Red thorns
Catch our clothes,
The scent of trampled plants
follows our passage.
Fortunately they are useful
for the cooking tripod.
May you be able, my master,
to bend down and choose
the perfumed seeds.

(P'ie Ti, *c.* AD 8)

XII

Quinces

Onomatopoeic words like *crash*, *bang*, and *squeal* sound like what they stand for. But there are also words which sound like the taste they represent. *Quince*, a contraction of the mouth, a suggestion of sucking the palate. An astringent fruit, but the name has beauty and a certain distinction. One wonders whether the names of certain fruits sound pleasant because the fruits have a pleasant taste. Take *apricot* for instance. This seems to me to be intrinsically a very beautiful word, just for the sound of it, and not only because its ripe cadence recalls the tawny redness of the fruit you have plucked to eat. *Fruit* itself is a lovely word, like so many English words containing an *r*. *Rosemary*, 'and we in *dr*eams behold the Heb*r*ides.' Observe the relation of *d's* and *r's* in those famous lines. Or *ripe*: '*R*ipeness is all.' It suggests a sort of summer fullness, a contentment we see in the eyes of some married women which tells of a great lewdness, greatly satisfied. I know there is more to it than mere sounds. We cannot hear a sound which is *only* a sound, else why is *wrack* beautiful and *rack* not? And like the baseless fabric of a vision, leave not a wrack behind. A filigree of spider webs, wisps of cloud after a storm. Rack? Something you do to heretics or from which you dust off the mouse droppings.

Behind our farm cottage there is a furrow of clear water beloved of frogs and black crabs, above which, as is proper and traditional, there is a quince hedge about twelve feet high. I have often been warmed by a quince hedge, since it was customary to cut from it a springy cane for up-ending small boys. It is a very tough wood, and *if* you can find a straight piece it makes a good staff. My great-uncle and aunt each had one, as yellow as their age. Concealed in the hedge is a hut without a door. In the spring lovely shell-pink blossoms come inside, as evanescent as your last meal; and in the autumn you can, when *in situ*, just reach out a hand for a lovely fragrant globe.

A large ripe quince is an attractive fruit to hold. You pull it off its springy twig and wipe off its faint covering of down. Its clear yellow suggests transparency, and it has a tangy, haunting fragrance. But it is somewhat forbidding too, for it is slightly knobbly and never really soft. As children we liked to eat them, but that liking usually departs with advancing years and leaves only the doubtful pleasure of nostalgia. Its taste is somewhat wry.

However, cooked in various ways it becomes very companionable. It does not cut as easily as an apple. Round the centre it is somewhat hard and granular. The pips are enclosed in a stiff bluish jelly which, as children, we loved to suck. Continue cutting up your quinces until you have a pile of small wedges, put them in a pot with very little water, a few pieces of stick cinnamon and some brown sugar. Stew them gently until they are a rosy pink and serve with cream. Even the granular centre softens quickly.

For jam one follows the usual procedure. I prefer to lay the chips for a few hours in lightly salted water before boiling. Quince jelly is, in my experience, excelled only by *amatungulu*[1] jelly with kei-apple[2] jelly as a runner-up. For the jelly you must use the fruit with peels, pips and all. Cover with water, boil till soft, strain by hanging in a jelly-bag overnight and cook with a pound of sugar to a pint of liquor — if you wish you can sieve what remains in the jelly-bag and boil the mush with sugar, which will give you either a pleasant spread or a fruity mousse for certain cooking jobs. You can also mix quinces and crab apples with *amatungulu* and add some good honey.

Or you can bake them. Baked quinces are excellent. Cut a deep hole into the core, and into it put sugar or honey, cloves and a date. Serve warm with cream.

When I see the first quinces of the autumn I always anticipate quince and mutton curry. Somehow Cape curries call for quinces. They make a good curry accompaniment in the form of a sambal.

1 *Carissa grandiflora*, a shrub with red, plum-shaped fruit and a tart strawberry/apple flavour
2 *Dovyalis caffra*, has bright yellow or orange fruit and acidic flavour

Grate ripe quinces, salt them lightly and let the moisture drain off for an hour. Then mix in a little brown sugar, oil, green chilli, pepper, vinegar, or better still tamarind juice and a little chopped mint. Leipoldt[3] gives a recipe for quince stew, using fat mutton, though I have not tried it. Follow the usual procedure for a *bredie* or stew. First brown the mutton with onions, add the quince and whichever herbs you fancy, salt, pepper, brown sugar and a dash of vinegar or dry red wine, and simmer for a long time. Stews must always stand for a long time so as to marry the ingredients.

Fruit should be prodigally used in cooking. When we have a case of cooking apples a great many of them go into the pots. Last night we had beef stewed with onions, potatoes, carrots, chopped apples and quinces and Swiss chard. Add pepper, salt, nutmeg and shredded sweet peppers. Try sliced apple fried with your bacon and eggs. And here is a scrumptious dish for lunch: Using a deepish covered pan,

3 Christiaan Frederik Louis Leipoldt (1880-1947), South African journalist, novelist, poet and cook

lay down a layer of rashers of bacon, then of sliced onions, then of sweet peppers, then of sliced apple or quince, and finally of tomatoes. Add pepper, salt, oil, a light sprinkling of brown sugar, and a little vinegar or dry wine. If you wish to make this a really filling dish, put in a layer of thin potato slices. Garnish with chives and fennel or basil.

Quince jelly is usually served as an accompaniment to roast meat or game. So are stewed, dried peaches. You can make an unusual accompaniment by taking a can of sliced quinces or peaches and blanching some thinly sliced onion in the heated syrup. Then put all together with a little chopped mint, and if you find this too bland, mix in a little grated green ginger or a small pinch of red pepper.

A dish of ripe, yellow quinces on the table, amongst which you have propped a few scarlet hibiscus blooms, both looks and smells splendid.

XIII

Potatoes

There is a certain romance even about a supermarket. It is a point at which the ends of the earth meet. Here are cloves and nutmeg from the Spice Islands, vinegar from the vineyards of France, Brazil nuts, olive oil from Greece and soy sauce from China. Such commodities are travellers and tell many tales to the imaginative ear. Odysseus carved his bedpost from an olive tree, and sesame evokes the Arabian Nights[1]. Some things did their travelling long ago, and have now settled down. The potato seems to be a real dumpy stay-at-home, and tomatoes have been flaring in our gardens for many generations. Yet they have not always been with us, having crossed over in the caravels of Spain, not long after Montezuma[2] drank his frothing *chocolat* in his palace and the men of

---

1   Medieval Persian literature, compiled by Abu abd-Allah Muhammed el-Gahshigar in the 9th C.

2   Moctezuma II, leader of the Aztecs

Cortes[3] ate maize cakes on the causeways of Tenochtitlan[4]. The Spaniards brought back gold and silver, to the ultimate ruin of Spain's economy. But their real treasure, their vegetable treasure, was such that it could have sunk their ships a million times over. Ferdinand and Isabella would not have been amused had they been given a potato instead of an emerald. They had not yet discovered it.

Potatoes are *Solanacae*, a vast family that includes, amongst hundreds of varieties, eggplants, peppers and tomatoes. One must remember not to plant tomatoes where potatoes have just been lifted.

But besides being a member of a large clan, the potato has become international, together with plants like lucerne and tomatoes. The sun never sets on potato eaters, and where the potato has taken root it has become one with the soil and the people. One does not ask where it came

3 Hernán Cortés, the conquistador who conquered Mexico for Spain

4 Capital of the Aztec empire, situated on the site of what is now Mexico City and largely destroyed by Spanish conquistadors in the 1520s

from because it seems always to have been there.

It has become international through its ability to become localised, that is it has been able to go everywhere because it can thrive in any spot. It can go everywhere because it is satisfied to be where it is. That is true internationalism, which is a kind of sublime local patriotism because it goes places and does not merely traverse spaces. To be able to be at home where you are is the pre-eminent requirement for being at home in other places. If you cannot be at home with yourself, you cannot be at home with other people. The abstract internationalism of mere space has no holding ground for any anchor. We talk about conquering space, that is dominating a something which is not a 'there.' But what shall it profit a man to gain space if he loses place, or to get to the moon if he can be evicted from his house? That is why jet aircraft meals do not feed you, but only a passenger, and why in these days of quick communication you are a taxpayer rather than a citizen. A lot of your money goes into space-devouring projectiles which are quite incredibly cerebral. The generalising reason is the murderer of substance. But it teaches you to preserve and transport foods, and make a profit doing so, so that a cloud of aliens is hurried from place to place but never belongs anywhere. Just as buildings tend to look alike nowadays in every city, so does the food in them taste the same. A democracy of food comes into being in which all foods are equal and universal. Perhaps our rapacious democracy will result in our all eating krill, if in the meanwhile we have not poisoned the sea, for poison, too, is international. Well, we must be polite to strangers, but have a brotherly feeling for the potato because he has his naturalisation papers. Have bird's-nest soup as a guest at your meals, but live on potato soup. One of my more disreputable friends declares: You cannot sleep with all the women in the world, but you ought to try. Likewise, and otherwise, you cannot taste all the dishes in the world but a bit of home cooking may in the end give more satisfaction. Frau potato may teach us all we need to know. Men may learn about women from her. Eating spiced harlot is not really satisfactory, however decorative the tin.

I do not wish to underrate the problems of assimilation. Since we have 'conquered' space they are more acute than ever. This holds not only for food and cooking. Medieval European art and religion were somewhat confined, but in exploring a relatively narrow set of themes they explored them well. By 1500 one could paint a woman with a child. But the modern painter has the art of all the ages and of all places at his disposal. How is he to ingest it? What must, say, the Catholic's attitude be towards Buddhism, Sufism and Zen, not to mention all that anthropologists have thus far unearthed? One has Basho's[5] haiku as well as Shakespeare's sonnets. Must one also have a *radong*[6] in one's orchestra, or turmeric or soy sauce in one's gastronomic compositions? I am all for casting a very wide net. The cook is also seeking the

5   Matsuo Basho (1644-1694), renowned Japanese poet of the Edo period

6   Obscure musical instrument

brotherhood of man, and if a new culture comes into being, his art will reflect it. And after all, it is not all that difficult to know not to put turmeric on your strawberries. What we should try to achieve, however, is not the cooking of space, but of place. There is no harm in space-cooking now and then, as long as it does not displace the here and now.

Local traditions are primary and, I hope, not easily displaced. Were you to give the same materials and instructions to a Cape Malay woman and an English housewife, I'm pretty sure the results would be different. However, let us get down to the potato *in actu exercito*, that is in the pot or just emerged from it.

Plain boiled potatoes are generally regarded as material to be further operated on, or merely one of many at a meal. Before considering this further, let us state an absolutely fundamental principle of cooking: Whatever you cook must be itself. It must be presented in its 'suchness', and with an enhancement and not a concealment of its essence. This is the due, not only of potatoes, but also of human beings. The central effort of every man is to become what he is, and properly humanised cooking reflects this in the respect it pays to its materials. Apicius's efforts to make things taste like other things is a condemnation of much in Roman society. The attempts of vegetarians to deceive you with bean cutlets is the homage vice pays to virtue.

Now a plain boiled potato really is something, if you have treated it right. The first crime you can commit against it is to peel it with a knife. Firstly it is wasteful. Weigh the peelings and convince yourself of the fact. Secondly it means you are taking away the delicate nutty flavour of a good potato. There are three things you can do instead. Boil your potatoes in their jackets and then pull off the skins or, if you must peel them first, use the carrot scraper which peels very thinly. In fact, if your potatoes are very fresh, you need only rub over them with a potscourer. Properly boiled potatoes are, to the discerning, a main dish. Split them open, insert a dab of butter and a pinch of salt, and have them with creamy milk. Grated cheese and parsley will do no harm, but are not necessary. Observe that letting a potato taste like itself does not mean that you should not process it, as when you boil it, nor that you shouldn't use additives. The essential potato is the humanised potato. A porcupine does not really eat potatoes because he cannot ennoble them. A potato is only a potato when you can give it a name. The first potato was created by Adam when he bestowed an accolade on it.

Let us complicate its life a little more. Cut a sufficiency of potatoes into small cubes and boil them in stock, with or without a chilli. Take them out and add to them an onion finely sliced, two tablespoons of mint or a tablespoon of basil, a little garam masala, salt and pepper to taste, and finally a cup of yogurt or mayonnaise or oil and vinegar. A really good tart vinegar goes well with potatoes, here and elsewhere.

This can be served cold as a potato salad, or hot with a dressing of oil, vinegar and nutmeg. This is one of those good basic recipes on which one can build, especially when it comes to the hot dish.

Try slicing a red pimento into it — red for the sake of the colour — or stirring an egg or two into the potato, or folding in anchovies or a bit of smoked snoek[7] or tunny[8]. If you put your mind into your palate, quite a vista of possibilities opens.

Here is a suggestion for a potato curry which dispenses with meat. Take a kilo of potatoes and two big onions, cutting both up roughly. Put them into a saucepan with three cups of stock and raise to the boil, adding a chilli or a pimento or both, garlic to taste, a few thin slices of green ginger, some stick cinnamon, salt, a little brown sugar and a splash of vinegar or lemon juice. Other vegetables can be added.

Here is another one in which potatoes play an important role. Parboil some big thinly sliced potatoes in stock, and reserve. Use a large covered pan, and wet the bottom with olive oil. Cover the bottom with strips of bacon, covering the bacon

---

7 *Thyrsites atun*, thin perch-like fish of the southern oceans with a taste similar to that of mackerel

8 Any of several oceanic fishes resembling mackerel

in turn with sliced onions; then cover the onion with your potatoes and the potatoes with sliced brinjal; now cover the brinjal (aubergine or eggplant) with sliced sweet peppers. This you salt and pepper, sprinkle with a good vinegar and dot with butter. If you like, you can top with a spicy pancake after everything has been simmered till soft.

One should always remember that there is no such thing as a good recipe in the abstract. It is relative to people and to circumstances. In some company you may wish to present a dish with a certain panache, or to use ingredients which are a status symbol. There are those Ionic dishes which Plato couples with girls from Corinth[9], curious in their arts. Joshua Slocum, in that best of sailing books, *Sailing Alone Around the World*, speaks of 'a sailor's most highly prized luxury, a barrel of potatoes', and though it may not satisfy a pig from Epicurus's sty, I have no doubt that in circumstances like these

9 Ancient Greek prostitutes employed at the Temple of Aphrodite

grilled flying-fish and potatoes would be just right. For the notion of a good recipe one should perhaps substitute the notion of the best performance with the ingredients available.

Good cooking is to produce, from what is given, something which is enjoyed. It satisfies hunger and promotes conviviality. To me a recipe does not start with 'First catch your hare', but rather with 'Invite John and Marion for lunch.' Cooking is an act of courtesy.

This is something which is well grasped in the East. A good cook must have got rid of his ego. A dish, however brilliant, which is a manifestation of his ego is bad. It will fail to be itself, which is what is wrong with the egoist. That is why a Zen monastery requires that its cook should be enlightened. If you do not understand this, you cannot understand the Japanese tea ceremony, nor how it could deeply influence a whole culture. You are giving a cup of tea. *Giving*, not showing off your china, or angling for a favour, or establishing an obligation, or concealing your real feelings. And the tea is *tea*, not a symbol for the wants of your ego. It comes over in its suchness. It is not alienated from itself, because your host is not; therefore it is not only a thirst quencher but a spiritual healer. So the recipe for tea starts: First catch your God and pop him in the teapot so that the tea may manifest its Buddha nature. That art thou. At bottom you and the tea are one reality, and your tea party is a real *convivium*. This is the real domestic science: an *itinerarium mentis in Deum*, a journey of the soul to God. After all, heaven is a *domus*, a home. To have tea with your guru will teach you more about cooking than Brillat-Savarin[10], whose *Philosopher in the Kitchen* is not philosophy at all but the record of a wallow, though we must grant that his trough was well spiced. Rather read Jack Santa Maria's *Anna Yoga*, the yoga of food.

If you perhaps think that I myself should come nearer home than black tea with butter and salt, let me quote this from the

10 Jean Anthelme Brillat-Savarin (1755–1826), French lawyer, politician, epicure and gastronome

medieval English mystical treatise, *The Cloud of Unknowing*[11]:

'You will ask me, perhaps, how you are to control yourself with due care in the matter of food, and drink, and sleep, and so on. My answer is brief: "Take what comes." Do this thing without ceasing and without care day by day, and you will know well enough with a real distinction, when to begin and when to stop in everything else. I cannot believe that one who goes on in this work with complete abandon, day and night, will make mistakes in mundane matters. If he does, he is, I think, the type who will always get things wrong.'

Perhaps you find this a bit much? I did, so I went to the kitchen, took three cups of meal, with salt and baking powder, moistened this with whey, patted it into four little loaves and put them on the stove in a greased frying pan. Where they will burn if I become too absorbed in what I am writing.

11 14th C. spiritual guidebook by an anonymous monk who trains a young student to seek God through love, not knowledge

Let us take leave of potatoes with this one. Let us call it smoked sausage with potatoes. It makes a pretty good meal.

Lightly braise your smoked sausages with some carrots cut in thin fingers, and some leeks. Parboil some nice mealy potatoes and parsnips.

In a heavy pot or deep, covered pan put some tailfat or oil and braise some diced pork in it. Then put in two sweet peppers cut in strips and a bay-leaf. Throw in a mug of good stock and put in your sausages, leeks and carrots, and your potatoes and parsnips in sizeable chunks. Now add pepper, salt, grated green ginger, a dash of good wine vinegar, and a heaped tablespoon of mint, basil or parsley. Stir this together, finish off with a grating of nutmeg and simmer for twenty minutes with the lid on.

You will be relieved to hear that the loaves did not burn. They are to be eaten hot with fig jam, which you make like this: Pull the skins off two and a half kilos of ripe figs. Put them in a heavy pot with half a cup of water, some root ginger, not powdered ginger, three quartered lemons and a tiny pinch of salt which cuts the too bland sweetness of any jam, especially apricot. When the fruit is well boiled, add two kilos of sugar and boil until the syrup begins to set — probably about half an hour. Fish out the lemon and bottle the figs.

XIV

A Short Disquisition
on Spinach

The mention of spinach may still cause the elevated eyebrow in some households. My little gardening encyclopedia, however, after dwelling on its healthfulness, declares that 'all classes should grow it.' Charmed as I am by this liberality of attitude, I have never been able to make healthfulness a prime consideration. That can be left to the domestic scientists who can undernourish and poison you as well as anybody else. I read not long ago of a man who died of vitamin poisoning. He had been captivated by what he had read concerning the healthfulness of carrots. You must remember that science endeavours to describe its realities, but that it can't live up to them. A good deal falls through the mesh. After all, it is not so very long ago that vitamins were not mentioned at all in describing carrots. A scientist does not have a God's-eye view of a carrot, nor of anything else. On this account it is best to rely on the culinary traditions of mankind and to trust to the fact that experience has always mended the worst holes in the mesh. Animals get along very well without test-tubes. What is good for them is what they like. Unfortunately we have lost a good deal of contact with our animality through being mesmerised by the remarkable powers of conscious reason. If it is true that our bodies have come into being through millions and millions of years of interaction with the world, then they represent a vast fund of experience on which it would be wise to learn to rely. That is what Lao-tzu means when he says that we underestimate the wisdom in stupidity. Cook by Tao and not by test-tube.

All this amounts to saying that our prime criterion in cooking should be what is nice and satisfying, leaving the vitamins to take care of themselves, which they usually do. This should be our attitude to spinach.

But spinach is a name for a lot of things,

an *omnium gatherum* of all sorts of foliage. You can 'make' spinach of lettuce, Chinese cabbage, turnip tops, and, of course, *Spinacia oleracea*, which all classes should grow. New Zealand spinach or *Tetragonia*, a somewhat succulent creeper, is very good, and once established has to be restrained rather than encouraged. If you are determined to go by mineral content, you will use nettles. The great Tibetan saint and poet, Jetsun Milarepa, lived for many years in a cave on Mount Kailas on nothing but. There is a very common summer weed called purslane[1] that makes a superb spinach. A couple of days ago I was able to point out to friends that they had a splendid meal growing out of the pavement in front of their house.

Purslane with mutton: You can make this dish as you would a stew of *water-blommetjies*[2] or water hawthorn. That is, you brown pieces of fat stewing mutton and onion in your heavy pot. Take the tips

1 *Portulaca oleracea,* aka Little Hogweed or Pusley, an annual native to India and the Middle East

2 'Water-flowers' in Afrikaans, *Aponogeton distachyos*, is a traditional Cape delicacy high in minerals and vitamins

and leaves of your purslane — it looks a good deal like the garden Portulaca and is equally succulent — wash them, mix them with smallish cubes of potato and allow to simmer. Finish off with a squeeze of lemon, salt, black pepper and a grating of nutmeg.

The favourite spinaches in our household are beetroot leaves and Swiss chard. Beetroot is the nicest, and probably best done very simply, that is steamed in a little stock with a squeeze of lemon. Swiss chard is a great space-saver in the garden since it can be cropped very frequently, and if sown and planted out in late spring will not bolt but grow on for a year. The thick white stems braise very well with a little oil and shredded bacon and should already be softened when you put the chopped leaves in. That is one very simple way of doing spinach. You can throw in a sprinkle of sultanas early on, and top with sliced hardboiled egg and nutmeg. Pepper and salt *q.s.* It is an excellent dish for a light lunch. You can play all sorts of variations on this, adding anchovies, for instance, or broken-up Maldive fish[3], bokkoms[4] or salted shrimps, or you can top your dish with a pancake or an omelet done with herbs.

If you prefer *sancta simplicitas* (O holy simplicity!), for which there is often much to be said, and if you don't have the Roman taste for disguising what your material is (which is why I consider Apicius a bad cook) then you will stir-fry your spinach in the Chinese way. Into your wok put half a cup of good vegetable oil, wash and drain your spinach well, put it in the hot oil, salting immediately, and stir for three minutes.

From the Mediterranean we get a recipe which makes of spinach a one-dish meal. For four or five people, take two pounds of spinach and cook in as little water as possible. Drain it and let it stand. In a capacious, deep frying pan heat olive oil in which you brown some minced garlic. To this add a small handful of seeded raisins, ten each of green and black olives, minced,

3   Spicy tuna fish preserve
4   A delicacy of heavily salted, dried mullet made along the West Coast of South Africa

a dessert-spoon of capers or nasturtium[5] seeds pickled in brine and vinegar, and half a small cup of pine kernels or slivered almonds. Then put in a small tin of anchovies. Finally add the spinach and fold in the other ingredients. Be careful how you salt, as some of the ingredients are salty.

Quite a nice and economical spinach pie can be made by putting spinach, cooked with a little oil or butter, into a baking dish. Now this is where you can use up that brown bread you are afraid may go stale. Soak some thick slices of bread in milk, salt and pepper, and crumble with a raw egg, chopped onion and chopped parsley. Work these together well and cover the spinach with it. You can put sliced tomato on top if you wish. Bake until it is all heated through.

5 Literally means 'nose-twister,' common name of the *Tropaeolum* genus of plants, native to South and Central America

XV

Homage to Moitjie

Moitjie is, and for very many years has been, our Malay washerwoman who comes veiled to us every Wednesday morning as regularly as sunrise. She is the quintessence of goodness, the main counter to my scepticism about 'good people.' You see, she never 'does good.' She is a descendant of those Malays sent to the Cape by the Dutch East India Company because they opposed the greed of the Company, which was enough to make them qualify as political prisoners. They have repaid this rape ever since by their contribution to the Cape culture as exemplary Muslim citizens. Moitjie is very observant and keeps the long fast without a murmur, working long hours in the heat without refreshment and restoring one's belief in religious discipline. Somehow she transcends the Qur'anic[1] literalism of the imams.

1   Al Qur'an Al Karim, Islamic holy scripture, a revelation from Allah to humanity, given to the Prophet Muhammad *c.* 610 CE

She doesn't 'do good', she *is* good. For one thing she is a superlative washerwoman and will take work from you rather than jib at any. Anybody who washes your clothes, washes your body, and when you wash the body you wash the soul. When she has been here we feel better, which is more than I can say for the washing machine. The abolition even of service is abolished along with it. After all, if you look at it theologically, self-service is pretty diabolical. Rather reign in hell than serve in heaven. Try it in your local supermarket, which exists, of course, only to do you good. When politicians, business men or financial corporations — they come to much the same thing — talk of serving you, button up your wallet. There are no free offers that do not endeavour to put a chain around your neck. I get a smile from Moitjie's toothless gums which really is gratis, and I have never heard her pass a moral judgment. This puts her in the class of saints far above the imams and the *dominees* (pastors).

She came to me the other day with a

little packet of spice for a biryani. It was good spice, and I know she couldn't really afford it, but like the widow's mite, it was just part of her aura. Malays are good cooks, and the best spread I have ever seen was put up by a Malay family. Wives, cousins, children, everybody comes together for a grand oblation[2] in the Eastern manner. So in praise of Moitjie I am going to tell you how to make *the* festive dish of the Cape Malays, a mutton biryani.

Parboil a kilo of rice, preferably basmati rice, salted, and melt a big spoon of butter into it. Put it on one side while you cut a fat leg of lamb into small bits which you must braise in a pot with some grated green ginger, plenty of sliced onion, crushed garlic, cumin and fennel seeds, and a pinch of *methi* (fenugreek). Don't cook the meat completely. Hard-boil three or four eggs.

In a heavy iron pot with a good lid put down a layer of rice, then a layer of meat topped with sliced egg. Repeat the layering until the pot is full. Dissolve a pinch of saffron in a cup of boiling water, spatter

2   Offering, such as worship or thanks, to a deity

179

it over the biryani, and dot with butter. Saffron is expensive, but no saffron, no biryani. It is the queen of all spices and gives the festive touch.

Cook this on very low heat for at least two hours, and bring the pot sealed to the table, where the lifting of the lid will envelop the company in a heavenly aroma.

Note on an Oriental aroma:

'We discovered The Aroma, described in the local English language newspaper as "the only deluxe restaurant in Nepal". I asked the manager why he had given the place this name. "Because," he said, fumbling for the English word, "it stinks good, yes?" ' (John Morris[3]) It reminds one of Coleridge in Cologne: 'I counted two and seventy stenches, all well defined, and several stinks.'

---

3   Author of *A Winter in Nepal*

XVI

Curry, Cuisine and Culture

One cannot separate the way people eat from the way they work and pray. Prayers frequently take the form of food offerings, as when Christians offer the bread and wine, or Hindus do *puja*[1]. As for work, primarily we work to eat, to feed ourselves and our families and friends. It is absurd to think of eating as a sort of fuelling-up process necessary to enable us to go off and do other quite unrelated things. There are no unrelated things. Man is man in an environment, and eating is one of the principal forms of commerce between ourselves and the world. It is also a principal factor in constituting our relations with other people. I must insist again that there is a great deal of truth in the saying that man is what he eats. He carves his surroundings into shape with his teeth. If I survey the landscape in my own

1 Ritual daily devotion involving offering of food, drink and prayers to a deity

region, I observe how the arable land has been worked over to produce food. There are areas under vines, others under fruit trees and still others under grain and pulses. You see numerous farmhouses and labourers' cottages, roads for the transport of produce, large factories and co-ops where the produce is converted into wines and tinned foods. Perhaps you remember the smoke-blue mist of olives on some Tuscan or Ligurian hill. No belly, then no entrancement of peach blossom in spring.

Or regard some exploited landscape where the soil has been mined and destroyed. It has been preyed upon by those who live by preying upon others. The real cannibals in the modern world are to be found in city boardrooms, and their wine will be trodden from the grapes of wrath. Dustbowls in the earth are signs of dust-bowls in the body social.

If you want to understand a people you must understand its food production, cooking and eating. Cuisine is closely tied up with religion, philosophy and art. If you wish to study Chinese thought you must

take an intelligent interest in Chinese agri-
culture and cooking. Approach Chuang-tzu
with a Chinese cleaver: so simple, sharp
and efficient. The ecumenical problem
is the problem of how to eat with others,
how to borrow ingredients and techniques
from others and how to be ethnic without
being exclusive. The possibility of living
on American bread is not unrelated to the
question of living with Americans.

The cuisines of the world come together
at the southern tip of Africa, a fact which is
part of my philosophical life. I happen to
be interested in Indian thought, and since
there are many Indians in South Africa, I
have been open to instruction on the art
of curry by a girl of South Indian origin,
in the course of which my pronunciation
of 'Upanishad' has also been corrected. Let
me give you an account of the most recent
demonstration.

Curry powder, let me say, is out.
Apparently it is merely a way of conning the
dumb foreigner. You don't make curry by
dumping a spoon of curry powder into an
ordinary stew any more than you become

superior to the 'mere' Christian tradition by throwing in an Om or a mantra at the right spot. So let us get to work with a good heavy pot into which you put some oil or butter, in which you braise finely sliced onions, and bay and curry leaves. Have you ever met a curry leaf? Tom Stobart in his *Herbs, Spices and Flavourings* tells you that in the game park in Kumaon[2] you can crash odoriferously through curry bushes while your elephant flushes out tigers. My curry leaves come from the Atlas Trading Company in Wale Street in Cape Town, though I am trying to grow some out of a sense of philosophic dedication.

You must now add your pile of chopped-up meat, mixed with plenty of macerated garlic and toasted coriander and green ginger. The meat is usually chicken or lamb, though bad people like the author have been known to use beef and pork. This is lightly browned, and to it you add coarsely chopped potatoes, a couple of tomatoes and, if you like, green beans. Salt

2 Mountainous region of Uttaranchal, a state of northern India

with sea salt.

Somewhere in the course of the proceedings you will have finely ground some cinnamon, cloves, coriander, cumin, fennel, several dried red chillies and a couple of cardamoms. Even a good Indian woman is not above using a spice grinder instead of a flat stone. To this you add some turmeric and a few chopped green chillies. Puddle it all in water and pour over the meat. The curry must boil briskly, until it has been thickened by the onions and potatoes, and should then be allowed to stand for a bit. While it is meditatively composing itself, chop up some green coriander or *dhania*[3], which can be bought here and there, or very easily grown by raking some ordinary commercial coriander into a garden bed. This you strew over the curry when you hot it up to serve. We curry snobs regard it as a must. Curry is best served with basmati rice. Brown rice, my instructress says, is for the birds.

This gives you a pukkah South Indian

3 Coriander seed powder

curry which I must admit tastes as divine as the Upanishads. But however inspired all this may be, I am unable to be too ethnic about it. My French forebears prod me. I remember Moitjie's insistence on tamarind[4], and our Cape custom of putting fruit into things.

'There are nine and sixty ways of constructing tribal lays, /And-every-single one-of-them-is-right!'[5]

For instance: Take a kilo of stewing mutton, flank or neck, cut into smallish pieces, and brown in a little oil together with three large sliced onions. Add to this five crushed cloves of garlic and two sliced sweet peppers. If you want your curry stronger, use instead of the peppers a chopped chilli. Put in two sliced apples — quinces are even better — and mix together about a thimbleful of sliced-up green ginger, a good tablespoon of ground coriander, two large pinches of cumin

4 *Tamarindus indica*, also called Indian date, tropical Asian evergreen tree, originally from east Africa, with long pods containing small seeds in an edible pulp

5 Spoken by the Totem in Rudyard Kipling's 'In the Neolithic Age'

or fennel seed, and a dessert-spoon of turmeric. Mix these spices up in a cup of vinegar and water, in which is dissolved a heaped teaspoon of brown sugar. Better than vinegar in any curry is a cup of tamarind water made by mashing up some tamarinds in a cup of hot water and removing the stones. Add your spices to the meat, and let your pot simmer for at least two hours. Finally salt.

A handful of raisins is a good addition to some curries. Most curry recipes I know make little use of fruit, whereas I prefer fruity curries. A handful of dates is good, and so is apple, quince, banana or pawpaw. Slice in green bananas, skin and all. The addition of a cubed sweet potato improves consistency. It is a pity to put brinjals in the curry since they lose their identity. Rather stew gently in a pot with some salt and pepper and butter, and lay the slices on top of the curry when you serve it.

Curry accompaniments are legion. Grated coconut is usually welcome or you can put coconut milk in the curry. But here again fruit is very suitable, melon for instance, or figs, very ripe and straight off the tree.

Wines with the curry course? The most tolerable are late harvest or a sweet dessert wine. The latter is agreeable with a hot curry. But on the whole wine is best omitted. The proper drink to take with curries is yogurt, or one of the excellent fruit juice cordials now available. These blend with curries, whereas wine usually has to put up a fight.

Curry is always served with rice. Here are two recipes for rice.

In a pot put butter or oil, a pinch of fenugreek and a small, finely sliced onion. Heat these and pour in a mug of rice, stirring until the rice is coated. Sprinkle with salt and add 2½ mugs of boiling water. Allow to cook until the water disappears. We sometimes stir a small spoon of honey into the rice.

Yellow rice: Into 2½ mugs of boiling, salted water put a mug of rice. Add a teaspoon of turmeric, small handful of raisins and brown sugar to taste. This should be cooked until the water has disappeared. Yellow rice also goes very well with roasts. So, by the way, do stewed peaches, especially if you can get hold of old-fashioned brown, hard dried peaches made from peeled clingstones. These peaches are usually home-dried, and are not obtainable on the market because the public has persuaded itself that yellow, sulphurous peach halves are better.

Fish curries, too, can be very appetising. One should use a firm fish like tunny, yellowtail or katonkel[6].

First make a good, well-matured curry sauce. You can do this the day before, as this helps the spices to settle down to each other's company. In hot oil braise plenty of sliced onions, garlic, a few cardamoms, sliced green ginger and a splinter of cinnamon. Make up some chicken stock with stock cubes and pour this on the spices, adding sliced sweet peppers or chillies to taste. Mix a heaped teaspoon of turmeric with a good vinegar or lemon juice and a sprinkle of shredded coconut. Salt to taste.

6   Variety of barracuda, *Scomberomorus commerson*

Cut the fish into pieces, dip these in oil and fry until almost done. Put them into the hot sauce. Garnish with sliced tomatoes sprinkled with basil, chopped green fennel or parsley. Then, as Isaac Walton[7] would have said: Much good may it do you!

There is one curried dish for which beef does very well, and that is curried mince or bobotie. You make it like this: Soak coarse brown bread in milk. If the bread is good and coarse, the proportion used can be fairly liberal. Take a kilo of beef mince and knead the bread into it, adding two raw eggs, a teaspoon of masala, two green chillies, a teaspoon of turmeric, two grated apples, a little brown sugar and a dash of vinegar, salt and pepper. Lightly cook this in a big pan, stirring well. Now pack your mince into a baking dish with the surface good and level. When the top begins to brown, cover with sliced bananas. Whip two eggs into a large cup of milk with a pinch of turmeric, salt and a little grated lemon or *naartjie* (tangerine) peel and

7   (1593–1683) English author of *The Compleat Angler,* one of the most published books in English literature with over 300 editions

a dusting of nutmeg. Pour this over the bobotie and let it brown and set.

In these days of expensive meat — and Buddhism — one should pay some attention to vegetable curries, which can be very good. Let me give you one I made two days ago.

Use rice, quinces, potatoes and onions. Coat them with oil, cover with stock and raise to the boil. Now mix fenugreek, turmeric, a little sliced green ginger, cardamoms, sliced sweet peppers and chilli. Mix with a little brown sugar and a good vinegar and simmer for at least an hour.

On this, many variations can be played by using a considerable variety of vegetables. Parsnips, for instance, go very well. Again one can use a substantial proportion of dried beans, first boiled soft. Dry bean curry is very good, with or without meat.

The vegetable and fruit accompaniment, called sambals, goes very well with any curry. Usually the constituent fruit or vegetable — quince, apple, carrot, cucumber, beetroot — is grated or shredded, lightly salted and allowed to drain for an hour or two. Chopped chives or shallots can be mixed in and a dressing made of vinegar, oil, a little brown sugar, salt and black pepper. One endeavours to keep a sambal crisp, fresh and cool. Therefore one grates raw and not cooked beetroot for a sambal.

I make frequent mention of good vinegar. People take a lot of trouble with wine for a meal, and astonishingly little with vinegar. One should, of course, use wine and not malt vinegar, but it is not always easy to find. There are some imported vinegars which are good, and a mere splash of which is distinctive. Apple cider vinegar can also be recommended. You can get much pleasure from making up your own herbal and spiced vinegars. Take several bottles of wine vinegar. Into one put garlic, into another chillies, into a third, tarragon, and so on, to taste. They should then be left to stand for a few weeks. It helps to warm them by the fire or in the oven.

XVII
Cooking the Marvellous

This little meditation started off by my wondering why a spice growing in Sumatra should please my palate, why a bark from Peru should be good for my malaria, and why orchids are beautiful. In pursuit of an answer I read Huxley and Kettlewell's biography, *Charles Darwin and His World*. After a praise of Newton[1] for his secularisation of the cosmos, you find these words of eulogy on Darwin 'who banished not only miracles but also creation and design from the world of life, robbed God of his role of creator of man, and man of his divine origin.' This may be a reason for the esteem in which Darwin was held by Engels[2], but beyond that it does not seem to have much to do with the truth.

1 Sir Isaac Newton (1642–1727), English physicist, mathematician, astronomer, philosopher and alchemist; regarded as one of the most influential scientists in history

2 Friedrich Engels (1820–1895), German political philosopher, developed communist theory with Karl Marx

Darwin's scientific genius was rooted in his sense of wonder; and to get rid of God you must get rid of wonder. God is the great question and exclamation mark, and thus the origin of what sets science in motion. Darwin's work did not put an end to science. There is still the question of the origin of *The Origin of Species*. If the negation of God is to have any dignity one must get beyond the pleasure of a small boy in having heaved a brick through a windowpane. When St Augustine said that belief in an occasional miracle was less important than the perception that the whole world was a miracle, he was talking about a wonder like Darwin's. The secular is the miraculous. Even the deism attributed in the same paragraph to Newton would ultimately put an end to science. Our small boy playing with a clockwork engine is no paradigm for man the physicist.

The trouble with the doubters of the nineteenth century is that they did not possess the clarity we owe to Sartre. They could still have their cake and eat it. That is why they earned the contempt of Nietzsche, and why it was left to Sartre to draw out the full consequences of a consistent atheism, and to find a self-created world and man simply nauseous. Let me quote again some lines from Sartre which have been quoted *ad nauseam*. Roquentin[3] is sitting in a public garden contemplating a nobbly, inert root showing up above the soil:

'It was useless to repeat to myself: This is a root: it did not click in my mind. Its function did not explain anything: there was no connection between its function as root, as hydraulic pump, and this hard compact surface, like the skin of a seal, this oily, harsh obstinacy. The function explained roots in general, but this particular root, with its colour, its shape, its arrested movement, was beneath all explanation. Every one of its qualities leaked from it a little, overflowed, became partly solid, became almost a thing; every one of them was unnecessary in a root.'

3 Protagonist in Jean-Paul Sartre's existentialist novel, *La Nausée*, written in 1938

To which one might add:

'All these things — the chestnut trees, the bandstand, the statue by Villedo in the Laurel thicket — abandoned themselves to existing like those tired women who relax into laughter murmuring in a tired voice: "It is good to laugh." I saw that there was no halfway between nonexistence and this swooning over-abundance. If you exist at all, you have to exist to this point: to the point of swelling, of mouldering, of obscenity.'

Sartre represents this godless universe as gooey and obscene, exuding a sort of nauseous plasma. Things *are* superfluous: they overflow. They are so much more than a mere function. The root is a sheer function overlaid with disgusting superfluities. What a universe of sheer functions would be like is almost too horrific to imagine. One should notice the connection between function and generality. All roots as functions are the same, and what makes them particular is the overburden of disgusting extras. What is assassinated is the unique: this particular onion which I am peeling with delight — this marvellous unique being or concretion, the sense of which led St Thomas to maintain that every angel was a separate genus.

Now having an eye for the concrete and unique is by no means something one can deny Darwin. It is rooted in the English Christian tradition. He was an empiric, cautious in generalising, loving the Ten Thousand Things, entranced by the oddness and variety of this world. For life is a cornucopia emptied into the greatest depths of the sea and into the atmosphere above. Glory to God for dappled things. I have a notion that my coincidental affinity for Peruvian bark is due to the incredible largesse emptied upon the earth, which is itself superfluous. Had Darwin not been so tied to explanations in terms of linear causality, he would have been more vocal about the vast, incredible coincidence of all that exists contemporaneously. As for the orchids? Sheer fun and droll generosity

— and pleasure in the unique. God did not, like Sartre, kotch over the orchids. We eat really diverse things, not functions. It is the abstract functional way of thinking which tries to invent nutrition pills enabling us to go on functioning — what as, or what for?

It is this sequential way of thinking that gives us an entirely wrong idea of creation. We place it at a point in time. God *once* created and then let the scroll unroll itself by its own momentum. But as St Augustine already pointed out, time is not an abstraction or an empty hold-all, but the very procession of creatures. It is the substance of the Ten Thousand Things, and it is the presence of God to things. That is why there is no time like the present. If we would rid ourselves of the sequential bogey and see God as the eternal creator, the eternal presence, the spark of eternity in the Ten Thousand Things, we could arrive at seeing that the world was not once created but that it is created, suspended over the pit of non-being, at each and every moment. The orchid is alive because God is alive — and whimsical. If creation is an overflow, then what is made in God's image must itself overflow, and that overflow is the carunculation of the root, the colour of the orchid or the light of sunrise.

Hassid Zaddik[4] stood at the window in the early morning and, trembling, cried: 'A few years ago it was night and now it is day — God brings up the day.'

May I translate here a passage from my book *Klip en Klei* (*Stone and Clay*) which I have hitherto refused to translate:

'What sense does the beauty of one little gladiolus make to another? And what is the beauty of one moth to another? What does the one perceive of the other? Whether, and in what fashion, one moth appreciates the colours and patterns of another, we couldn't say. What can one flower "see" of another? We can write a poem about a moth, but moths don't write poems about each other. They blush unseen. Or don't they? Now and then we notice one, but what of the millions that are unseen? Or those which became extinct before man's

4   Tsadik, Hebrew for 'righteous one'

advent? Insects had their heyday millions of years ago, and nature is essentially a beauty which cannot be appreciated from within.

'If I ask myself why the moth is so beautiful, I can't answer "For the sake of other moths," because that already presupposes the moth. Nor can I say "For my benefit," because that attributes to me an absolute importance I cannot lay claim to. The moth is a gift, a present, to me. It has its own purpose and a secret which I cannot touch. It is as though a kind of radical unselfishness and generosity roots in nature so that nothing exists only for itself or even for its kind. The moth comes before our eyes as something which is gratis and superfluous, overflowing with characteristics to which no functional and utilitarian explanation can do justice. It glories in its uniqueness because it is quite superfluous, given to itself and to us as a sheer gift.'

The fallacy in popular Darwinism is that it is too broadly based on the notion of utility. This or that variation is *useful*. The splendour of the orchid, the quinine[5] in the bark, are useful for survival. Hence the notion of nature red in tooth and claw. Each bit of life is one ego trying to get in ahead of the others. Capitalist nature! The result is a nature shorn of all superfluity and largesse which turns into egoism the glory of humility with which the thing, the substance, celebrates its own being. What is fundamental in reality is not self-preservation but generosity. That is why nature is a *convivium*, and not merely an unstable equilibrium of utilities. The orchid does not become beautiful because of the prescience that otherwise I might destroy it. It is beautiful because it is an eternal superfluity presenting so many facets that it can hook up with the rest of the world in astonishing ways. That is how I can link up with Peruvian bark.

Our devastation of nature is a consequence of our not seeing this. We see it as a welter of struggles for domination,

5 Bitter-tasting, natural white crystalline alkaloid, with antipyretic, anti-malarial and analgesic properties

by imputing to nature our own lust for dominion. We create a chaos of egos, and see in nature the mirror of our own society, a cannibalism of egos. The basis of nature conservation is a vision of nature as superfluous, and therefore generous because created in eternal generosity. The man who does not grasp his own superfluity, his presentedness to himself, will have an ego which exploits other men and nature, for we cannot turn nature into a dust-bowl without doing the same to our society. The secret of nature and of the evolutionary process is humility, therefore we should see nature as play, as a great game rather than a grim struggle. If nature is, as St Augustine said, an order of love, we can expect anything to happen because love is creatively spontaneous. It is this spontaneity which is bodied forth in the evolutionary process. The *raison d'être* of our *convivium* is not work but play. Natural selection presupposes the rich efflorescence of superfluity, so perhaps we should call it natural appreciation. Nature looks more like a dance than a board meeting.

Evolution is what we eat, and if you go wrong about evolution you go wrong about cooking and you miss the glorious coincidences, cooperations and marriages marking the course of nature. Bacon and eggs — what a marriage! Pumpkins, potatoes, beans, carrots, parsnip, finocchio (Florence fennel), celeriac, chicory, tomatoes and eggplant — what a dance! They are differentiated, each is itself, because they have danced out of God, each in his own clothes, to make their contribution to the *convivium*, where marvellous meetings take place, and the dominoes often slip for new recognitions. The blue of the gentian is an act by which the gentian loves itself, for as St Augustine holds, every creature is like the Holy Trinity in that it is itself and knows itself and loves itself. The blue is also the act by which God loves it. And remember that you come into it too, for the blue of the flower is its blueness to you. It isn't blue except in your company. And the same holds for the gust of saffron or the bitterness of Peruvian bark. Therefore a recipe, which is a way in which you deal with the Ten Thousand Things, is also a lifestyle. If you can get your ingredients to be and know and love themselves, they will ascend as a sweet savour from the altar which is your dining table. A recipe is a lifestyle, and you can cook yourself into heaven or hell. A good cook creates pied beauty. Don't eat his dish because it is necessary, or full of vitamins, or not fattening, but because it is gorgeous. Then your eating can be in praise of God and of the togetherness of a company in the *convivium*. If your cooking is play and not work, it will smell of Paradise. The resurrection starts in the cooking pot, because man is what he eats and because what he is, his substantial existence, is in its uniqueness touched with eternity. He is so utterly superfluous and dispensable that he is lovable and will never be dispensed with. The water and wine and bread of life go into the privy, yet go with us beyond history. Nothing hits heaven which does not hit the earth.

XVIII

The Tycoon and the Pressure-Cooker

I admit that there is a pressure-cooker in our kitchen and that I often use it. There! I have made my confession, I am purged of my guilt, I can see both sides of the question.

I am not one of those who damn pressure-cookers without qualification. For the reduction of dried peas and beans and tough bits of soup meat to something edible I am all for them. But there it ends. You can't finish a soup in a pressure-cooker because it has a lid which prevents your hanging over the bubbling broth and throwing in this and that as imagination and occasion prompt you. This is a defeat of love. It clamps down on versatility — there are so many bredies you cannot make that way, and so it can usher monotony into the family cuisine. Let me put it this way: You can do quite good second-rate cooking, but no meals which are first-rate. This is quite high praise, because a B+ meal is not all that common. Still, excessive use of a pressure-cooker will cramp your style and ruin your art. If one has honoured guests one must not cook for them in a pressure-cooker.

The great argument in favour of the pressure-cooker is that it saves time. Its use is an index of our attitude to time. 'Saving time' is a curious phrase — you cannot keep chunks of it in empty jars in a cupboard. Saving time seems to me to mean using or enjoying or producing commodities we would otherwise be without. This is fair enough — it saves time when you buy a packet of needles or a lamp-bulb rather than try to make them. The division of labour is a way society has of dealing with time. A community which uses horse-drawn ploughs has a different time-scale from one using tractor-drawn disc ploughs. The question is: Does what I gain in timesaving outweigh the good of the activity I curtail or relinquish? It is immensely important to connect the notion of the division of labour with the notions of time and money. The division of labour necessitates exchange, and this in turn requires the use of money. I pay money for the time I save by not trying to make my own shoes. Bad government or tyranny is a theft of time and a perversion of the monetary system. It is easy to see how the notion that time is money came into being, and how people come to ask large sums of money for their time: My time is precious so don't you waste it. But time, like money, is an abstraction, an idol to which we can sacrifice human relationships by preferring lesser goods to better ones. It sacrifices the good time created by a division of labour, which looks to genuine human needs, to the bad time which is created when we manipulate commodities and therefore human beings for the sake of the money which enables us to have time for our wasted efforts and dissipations. There is a vast chasm separating what I call ego time, and love time, which gives us time to praise. Perhaps praise is a good synonym for eternity. The rush and bustle of the world goes together with the conviction that time is money, and when we have immersed ourselves in a time which has no end, that is in ego time, which wants to go on and on, we are in hell where we shall have no leisure to repent.

Hell, in fact, is tycoon time, the time stolen from others, so that they have to hustle more and more in order to live. The tycoon is the fellow who mass-produces pressure-cookers in order to give the housewife more time to do a job and have more time to be his secretary or packer or label-licker or what have you. He creates the do-gooder or activist-philanthropist who bustles round in the same kind of time, which is the time of hell. I doubt whether the readiness to pounce on any profit and the eager search for wrongs to be righted are very different. I have an evangelical cookbook which tells me to use teabags in order to have more time for doing good!

Salvation is to love something real rather than merely having an idea of right or of money or of liberty or whatever. Cooking is a great opportunity for love and therefore for salvation. Love the leisure of the simmering pot and the long-drawn-out thoughts of the people you wish to please. For God's sake don't throw a commonwealth of meat and vegetables into the pot and clamp the lid on in order to have time to look over the agenda for the next meeting. It is the love of ideas which makes us cruel and not the love of this bit of meat, these potatoes, this child or wife or husband. A friend of mine was consulting a well-known and busy medical man who carried with him an atmosphere of leisurely absorption in the affairs of his patients. One day my friend asked him: 'Doctor, how come you can treat me as the only person in the world when I know you have so many patients and so many duties to attend to?' The reply hit at the very core of reality: 'Well, you know, my parents loved each other.'

I once wrote an essay entitled *Persons* to show the ultimate identity of time and love. Love is having time for somebody or something. 'Making time' for something is an expansion of love. Be careful how you save time. It is our contraptions for shrinking time and space which occasion our hellish hurry. Eternity is simply having time for God, 'who knows how to act when resting.' A Taoist would say that sitting still doing nothing, the Tao does everything. Eternity is the patience of God; salvation, our surrender to his patience. Loving God, like loving any person, is having time for him, and the time for God is eternity. *Deus amor* (God is love) and *Deus sua aeternitas* (God is eternal) mean the same. Love and eternity are not juxtaposed words but interpenetrating beings.

Perhaps the way to heaven is learning to wait on somebody, in both senses of the term 'wait on.' Waiters are sometimes less dumb than go-getters. The arts of service and waiting have been eclipsed in the modern world by the advent of self-service, evolved by vendors who want quick returns through larger turnovers, arising from a more direct evocation of greed. The waiter brings you food. Self-service brings you cans.

Cooking may be a spiritual exercise, teaching us to wait on time and to trust